THE MARGOT FONTEYN ACADEMY OF BALLET

Basic Handbook

www.fonteynacademy.org

ISBN: 978-1-105-62604-3

This handbook contains your complete information on how The Margot Fonteyn Academy of Ballet operates. It is designed to aid families and students through their association with the Academy, giving clear rules, regulations, standards, practices, and requirements. It also presents an overview of our Educational Program, designed by Dame Margot Fonteyn de Arias in conjunction with Artistic Director Ken Ludden.

"Welcome to The Margot Fonteyn Academy of Ballet. This institution is designed to take talented children and shape them into the leading artists on the classical ballet stages of the world. The high level of our standards impresses upon our students the hard work, commitment level, dedication and principles needed to become a professional dancer. But here at the Academy we look beyond the years an artist is expected to be able to dance, and lay the groundwork for professional involvement in every aspect of the classical ballet theatrical companies of the world. Through this dedication to the whole life of the artist being formed in our classrooms, we seek to bring out the very best each student has to offer.

"Dame Margot believed that every dancer should have the benefit of formal education in the other art forms actively involved with ballet – music, drama and painting. This integrated form of education is as balanced as it is thorough. By completing this course of study, each student will have developed the skills, instincts and artistic integrity embodied by the legacy of Fonteyn, as she set the standard of excellence for all times in her own career.

"Welcome to our Academy."

Ken Ludden, Founder/Director

Table of Contents

Admissions

Entry into the Lower School is a three-part process: assessment, general test of dance knowledge, and an art exam.

The child must pass physical assessment by our staff to determine the structural makeup of the skeleton, musculature and overall physical suitability for classical ballet. They must demonstrate general knowledge of classical ballet positions, basic steps and terminology by taking an audition class. The art exam includes a written test, oral presentation and a presentation of a work of art. The physical assessment and audition class determine acceptability for entry to the Lower School. The art examination determines placement, not acceptability.

Those interested must fill out an application form (downloadable on this website, or call and have it mailed to you via post), and then schedule an interview. There will be audition classes for each level, and you must sign up for these classes in advance. Should your schedule prohibit attendance at a scheduled audition class, a private session can be arranged, but only in extreme circumstances. For some students, private instruction will be recommended, particularly if the child has had extensive previous training, have special needs, or need to catch up to the level of the ongoing class to enter it successfully. All of this will be discussed at the interview, and then a final determination will be made after the audition class.

Audition Class

Children will go through an audition process including at least one technique class. Should there be many candidates, or more candidates than there are spaces available, this may include one or more call-back auditions. The audition class is a basic ballet class and is used to determine the general knowledge of ballet positions, simple movements and an understanding of body mechanics. It is assumed children will have had prior training in the basics before entering the Academy.

For those who wish to enter and have had no prior training, a separate class will be held. This class does not assume any previous training, and determines the overall coordination of the child, their ability to learn and repeat physical movement instructions, and their natural ability.

Review Committees

Academy students must regularly perform before Review Committees at specific times in their student progression. Each Spring a Review Committee convenes for that year's Grand Défilé, and also for the danced portion of their final exams. Review Committees also are convened to arbitrate special circumstances, to adjudicate institution or reversal of certain expulsions, and to be able to matriculate to the next level. These panels will be formed at the time of the review cycle, and will draw from the Academy's Artistic Advisory Group, Mr. Ludden's personal contacts in the world of the arts, and other invited experts.

Audition Exam

Each student must take an exam that determines the child's ability to understand and relate to various forms of art. The audition exam is not one that can be passed or failed, but rather shows the Review Committee at what level the child is tuned in to the arts. In addition, each child will be required to create a work of art (drawing, poem, song, sculpture, movement piece) that is inspired by something in their own life experience. Parents must be sure to include in the application form a list of any and all art related studies the child has done.

Once a student is accepted into the Academy, they will have periodic exams in ballet technique, music and art. All students in the Academy will be required to do a basic study of music. Students who are studying musical instruments privately will receive a waiver from the study for as long as they are in this other regimen. However, all students will be expected to pass the music examinations that will be given periodically. Passage between levels requires successful mastery of different art forms, and is determined by a specific exam for the level being sought by the child.

Cumulative extra credit is awarded for ongoing study of a foreign language. This credit helps toward entry into the Upper School. Specialty classes will be offered (pointe, variation, partnering, men's technique) and will be recommended by the Head Master of the school for particular Lower School students when it is determined they are in need of that particular expansion to their work.

Physical and Psychological Assessment

Both physical and psychological assessments are made of each applicant. The physical assessment determines range of motion of major joints in the body; examines structure of head/neck, spine, legs, and feet; and considers at percentage of body fat and reviews eating, sleeping, exercise and health aspects of the child and his/her environment. The psychological assessment helps determine the temperament of the child and their suitability to the stresses and demands of an eventual career as a stage artist. This assessment is done by a certified psychologist, who will continue to track the development of each child through their work at the Academy.

Should the child be selected for the Lower School, they will receive a review of this assessment with recommendations for how their environmental circumstances might be enhanced to better support study of classical ballet.

Classical ballet technique is one of the most rigorous disciplines for the physical body. The basic stance in ballet has the legs rotated outward from the center - called turn out. This allows full freedom of movement, but also utilizes the smaller muscles of the body. The larger the muscle, the slower it works, so in dancing and other physical disciplines that require accuracy and speed of movement, more efficient use of the smaller muscles will produce a better result. Some people have natural turnout, others not. In the case of a child with no ability to move in this way, ballet is not appropriate to pursue.

Musculature

The feet in ballet must be very strong but also aesthetically shaped. Again, a naturally strong and beautiful foot is very important for classical ballet. Margot Fonteyn did not have "ballet feet" per se, for they lacked the extreme flexibility that makes a foot more visually impressive. Nevertheless, she became the most famous ballerina of all time, but this was due to hard work, and always working with acknowledgement of her assets and limitations. In the physical examination, the child's feet will be considered. There are some natural shapes of feet that preclude dancing in classical ballet, but are not prohibitive of a career in modern, jazz or show dancing.

Skeletal System

The spine, and the natural musculature of the back and neck are also examined. To dance well one must have strength, flexibility and a naturally good carriage. There have been many ballet dancers with mild or moderate spine curvature (scoliosis), but they have to work in specific ways so that they do not injure themselves. Those with spine disorders that prohibit ballet dancing will have that explained to them, and while they might not be able to join the Academy, they will be able to enter into some of the other programs offered in the Public Ballet division of the Academy.

Finally, the legs and arms are of vital importance as extensions of the torso, where all movement originates. Problems such as hyper-extension of the legs, double-jointedness, bowed legs, knock knees, etc., must be addressed.

Even in extreme cases some of these conditions are workable for ballet dancers, but there is a very specific way one must work to compensate. These children, if they meet the other requirements for entry, may have to have private class work in addition to their normal Academy schedule for the first year, or for as long as it takes to develop the muscles and awareness necessary to dance properly given their physical make up.

Dress for Physical Assessment

When you come for the physical assessment, the child should wear comfortable clothes that allow flexibility but also that are tight enough to see the muscles and skeletal structure. A fitted T-shirt and shorts are good, if the child doesn't already have tights and leotards. Girl's hair should be pulled up and secured so the neck and face are clearly visible.

Female Students

Introduction of Pointe Work

Female students will commence work on pointe only when directed to do so by their teacher. The proper technique of dancing on pointe requires full development of secondary and tertiary muscle sets, proper use of muscles to point the foot, and mastery of quarter-pointe techniques in balance and turning. To put a child on pointe before this is achieved will severely damage the muscles, cause bone damage and/or distortion, and lead to lumbar injuries.

Upon achievement of Level 3 status in the lower school, all students, male and female, are required to take one specialty class per week.

In the case of female students, this will most likely be a pointe class. However, some will not be ready, and they will instead be directed to take a character dancing class, or some other specialty class.

But by Level 3, all female students MUST take pointe class. Since the class requirement for Level 4 includes a pointe class, then, it is not possible for any female student to advance to that level unless she is able to dance *en pointe.*

Qualifications to begin Pointe

This does not mean a student not yet ready for pointe work will no longer be acceptable for Academy study, it just means she needs more time at Level 3 for her body, muscles and technique to develop adequately.

No child should be made to feel as if she has failed for this reason, even though it is natural to feel this way. Instead, if a particular female student is not developing as quickly to be prepared for pointe work as others, she may be directed to have some private classes to help her achieve this and keep up with the others in her class.

But there is absolutely no circumstance in which a child will be put ***en pointe*** before she is physically ready, as it might give her an injury or permanently damage her physique.

Male Students

The world of classical ballet needs many more male dancers coming through the ranks. The Academy will conduct constant educational and promotional events to expose young men to the idea of dance. Outreach programs into the school systems will be developed.

The Academy will also invite fathers to participate in father/son movement workshops (see Body Mechanics below). Due to the need for more male dancers, there will be different fees for male dancers in many cases, a variety of scholarships, and other programs to encourage and support enrollment.

The introduction of dance competitions and the impact of demi-character dancers in the classic prince role have altered the way male dance technique is taught. These new additions are spectacular and make for much better male dancers, but have eclipsed many traditional types of male dance steps, particularly petit allegro. At the same time, many contemporary choreographers have simplified the lexicon of dance vocabulary (the steps). It is currently believed that learning the full complement of dance somehow limits or interferes with the prowess of the male dancer in his current incarnation. In truth, however, the "competition" mentality that is common in many of today's male dancers does not prohibit the male dancer from performing the full complement of male technique. Male Academy students will be required to develop their full technique, particularly petit allegro, to remain enrolled in the Academy.

Male technique classes will be required of male students starting in Level 2 and throughout the rest of their work in the Academy, both Lower and Upper schools.

The Academy will conduct special classes and programs for male students. There will be special Body Mechanics workshops for athletes held regularly for male students (or female) who are athletes and wish to achieve the highest form of achievement within their sport. These workshops will be required for all male students of the Academy, and these students will be used as example in the workshops.

Dress Code

All children will be required to adhere to the dress code while in ballet class. Outside of class, there is no uniform or dress requirement.

Female Attire

All girls are required to wear pink (or natural skin tone per permission from Head Master), pink soft ballet shoes (with proper elastics). Hair is to be pulled back and put into a tight bun at the rear crown of the head. Other requirements are specific to level.

Level 1 – Black leotard (scoop neck). Long sleeves from October through April, short sleeves from May through September.

Level 2 – Royal Blue leotard (scoop neck). Long sleeves from October through April, short sleeves from May through September. Ballet shoes must have ribbons sewn on them in class at all times, never just elastic.

Level 3 – Ballet Pink leotard (V-neck). Long sleeves from October through April, short sleeves or cap sleeves from May through September. Matching pink decoration in hair upon approval. Ribbons on ballet shoes required. Point shoes if on pointe.

Level 4 – White leotard (V-neck). Long sleeves from October through April, short sleeves or cap sleeves from May through September. Matching white or pink decoration in hair upon approval. Ribbons on ballet shoes required, pointe shoes if on pointe.

Male Attire

All boys must wear white T-shirt, tight fitting, and have short enough hair that it doesn't go into the eyes. (If hair is longer (allowed in Level 4), then it must be secured to the head with a dark, solid-colored bandana.

Level 1 – Black tights with rolled belt, black canvas shoes.

Level 2 – Black tights with rolled belt, white socks and white canvas shoes.

Level 3 – Grey tights with rolled belt, white socks and white canvas shoes.

Level 4 – Off-white tights with crossed elastic shoulder straps, white canvas shoes. Hair may be longer but must be tightly bound to the head by a dark, solid-colored bandana.

Other Dance Attire

Leg warmers, if worn, must be tight fitting, match in color to the school uniforms and be easily removed. They will not be rolled or folded in any way that obscures the line of the body or its musculature.

Should it be sufficiently cold in the studio, sweaters can also be worn, but must fit tightly, or be secured by crossing ties. NO SKIRTS MAY BE WORN IN CLASS.

Performance Opportunities

Ballet is a performed art. Simply working in a studio is not enough to create seasoned dancers, ready for the professional stage. A very simple truth guides the student's progress: Performance Begets Performance.

Therefore, the Academy will create regular opportunities for students to perform. In addition to seasonal dance reviews performed for the general public, there will also be choreographic showcases, short danced video productions, and other opportunities for public performance. Students will have to audition for these productions on occasion, and other times will be assigned to perform. The Academy staff alone decides when a student is ready for performance. If it becomes known that a student has done any public performance without prior written permission from the Academy staff, they will be expelled.

In the case that a student is taking another performing art as their general art class (musical instruments, drama, singing, etc.), they will be allowed to perform in all public offerings directly related to the course work for these classes. But if a student is asked to perform by the staff of such programs, and that performance is not directly related to the course work, they will need written approval for such public performances prior to the event.

In the case that a student wishes to become registered with Central Casting or any other agency that arranges for performance-related work, a waiver must be signed by the Academy staff.

The Academy stands strongly behind public appearances, when the student is ready. The need for written agreement in these matters is not to restrict, but to teach proper business approach to public performance, assure that proper recognition of the student's work is clearly specified in any contractual agreement signed by student or parents, and to assure the highest standard of quality in all public performances.

Sports, Activities, Other Training Programs

The level of training at the Academy is very much like Olympic training, as it is the highest standard possible, and looks to a long future for the student. The level of physical development is such that the muscles must develop in extremely specific ways so that the student can have the level of mastery of the steps needed to meet global standards for classical ballet. Consequently, the type of outside activity must be limited so it does not contradict specific muscular development. The Academy recognizes that today's youth are encouraged to participate in sports activities. Many public and private schools recognize ballet training as equivalent to sports, but some do not. It is up to the student and his/her parents to understand the unique demands of classical ballet and be sure that nothing is being done to contradict or undermine the ballet training.

Ballet dance technique requires the dancer to use what is called “turnout”, which is the full rotation of the hips. The muscles that control turnout are small, and are located at the top of the leg, in the hip joints, and around the pelvis. Training the body to rely on these secondary and tertiary muscles takes time and constant exercise. To make these muscles strong enough to perform classical ballet steps well takes years of development. Any repetitive use of the large muscles of the legs (quadriceps and glutei maximi) will lead to their overdevelopment, and contradict the use of the smaller muscles. Therefore, any sport or activity that demands of the body to work constantly with the legs in a parallel position works against the ballet training. Track and Field, cycling, jogging, and knee bends are counterproductive to the child’s development.

Likewise, to achieve maximum efficiency of movement unencumbered is also an essential basic element of ballet technique. The dancer must have absolute control of every single muscle in the body, and know each muscle’s strength, range, flexibility and speeds. It must not be over developed, nor developed with artificial stresses or confinement, for if a muscle is confined or overdeveloped, it will not function reliably or properly. Just as the body must be free of unnecessary excess fat, so too must the muscles remain free of internal scar tissue because any extra weight slows the speed capacity of the muscle and interrupts the brain’s ability to communicate with that muscle. Therefore, weight training also works against proper development of the body for ballet.

We recognize that team sports can provide much benefit to children, can help in development of social skills, and give a child a sense of accomplishment that is widely recognized by their peers and society in general.

Should a child want to participate in school sports, they should be encouraged to do so. However, once an Academy student achieves a particular level of technical ability, the study of ballet must take precedence in their lives, and they will most likely be given athletic requirement credit for their work in ballet.

Sports Compatible with Ballet Study

Below is the list of sports that work well with classical ballet training:

Baseball	Squash
Softball	Racquet Ball
Basketball	Surfing
Billiards/Pool	Swimming
Diving	Synchronized Swimming
Equestrian	Table Tennis
Dressage	Team Handball
Hand Ball	Tennis
Fencing	Volley Ball
Field Hockey	Beach Volley Ball
Gymnastics	Water Polo
Polo	Wrestling
Soccer	

Academy students must consult the Director or Head Master if participation in a sport is of interest. It is recommended that the student, their parents and the coach of the sport have a meeting with Academy staff or Head Master to outline what is required by the sport, and to coordinate the sport training with the ballet training so there is no conflict for the developing body.

Body Mechanics Class

Body Mechanics is based exercises culled from ballet conditioning routines, teaching physics of movement, proper muscle use, and body coordination. They are divided into 7 basic principles of movement: propulsion, torsion, rotation, trajectory, absorption, impetus and inertia.

The Body Mechanics classes offered by the Academy also help understand the proper application of principles for a specific sport. Special Body Mechanics seminars are offered to sports teams MFAB students belong to, showing how dance training enhances sports performance.

GRADING

The grading system is geared to accurately assess the ability of each student in the same way the professional dance world assesses a dancer. Each year the students must prepare for the Grand Défilé, which is a public presentation of their work. The Grand Défilé is graded by a panel of five examiners, and their final grade constitutes one third of the grade for the year. Academic work for the year as a whole and the Examination Ballet Technique Class are the other two-thirds.

In the dance world, giving your all by going the extra mile is very influential in a career. Everything a student does that is extra (be it an answer to an exam question with more information than the minimum required, or extra reports or presentations of projects throughout the year) is given credit.

Showing up equals getting ahead more than anything else. The history of ballet is filled with stars who got their break because they chose to hang out, or stay and watch rehearsals, etc. In view of this, and as training by example, attendance is counted heavily. If a student comes to more classes than are required, they are given credit for the percentage more than require added to their final cumulative score for the year. Likewise, if a student is in attendance less, that percentage less than required is subtracted from their final cumulative score.

Tests

General Arts classes either have a final exam, a paper, or a project. These are graded by the teacher, and the comments are given as to the student's participation and contribution. Scores reflect the amount a student is ready to proceed to the next level of training at the Academy, rather than in competition with the class or with the test itself. Again, extra credit counts.

Projects

There are different projects at different times of the year. For example, students may be given the job of decorating the front display case for the studio, or selecting and arranging the photographs hung in our lobby. Students participating in such projects will receive extra credit for their work.

Final Exams

At the end of each school year there are two final exams for each student: the danced final exam, and the written final exam. The danced final exam score is worth a third of the student's final grade, before the adjustment for attendance.

Danced Final Exam

The Danced Exam is usually graded by a panel of three examiners and by the director of the school. Every element of each barre exercise is evaluated and scored. The maximum score is 2.0 for any one element, and each student begins the exam with a perfect score across the boards. As the examiners witness the execution of these exercises, they deduct .1 (a tenth of a percent) for each time the student falters in the particular element of the exercise. For example, if the student is doing grand plié, every time the knees do not line up with the toes, .1 is deducted from the score. Beginning and ending positions for each exercise are graded, and quality of movement as well.

In the centre floor exercises, examiners consider the combination of specific execution of elements of steps, as well as the general coordination, flow, quality of movement and expression of the exercises. The centre floor work is therefore taken both in parts and as a whole.

In addition to these categories, there are 14 overall qualities that are examined. These are: readiness before music begins, starting head position, starting body position, ending head position, ending body position, memory of exercises, response to corrections, musicality, clarity of execution, arm-body coordination, attention to detail, expressiveness, phrasing, and quality of movement.

Students are judged on execution of the exercises and these other qualities. There is no handicap awarded for the level a student is in, as every one of the qualities examined is requisite in dance movement at every level. The difference between levels is in the material given in the class, rather than the ability to do the exercises.

Written Final Exam

The Written Final Exam tests the entire body of knowledge taught at any given level, and is graded as percentage of readiness to matriculate to the next level. In the Lower School there are two tiers of General Arts curriculum, A and B, and each year the tier offered toggles between the two. Therefore, if a student has only attended the Academy one year, to receive 50% on the written final exam reflects a perfect score. This is doubly challenging because students must retain knowledge from year to year or they cannot pass the exam.

Matriculation

Proceeding to the next higher level in the Academy is a based on knowledge and performance. But in the Lower School there is the very important element of body development. Children cannot be forced to work at a level that their physical development cannot sustain (as in pointe work, partnering, fifth position, etc.). Therefore it is necessary that each student be considered specifically.

As a guide, however, when a student has an overall score between 95% and 99% before the attendance adjustment, they are automatically considered for the next level of the Academy. Issues of physical facility, and maturity level, are taken into consideration and discussed by faculty members. The director makes the final decision. If the student scores 100% or higher, they automatically matriculate unless there are serious factors prohibiting this.

No student scoring less than 90% in their General Arts can proceed to the next level without a written determination by a specially formed Review Committee.

Academic Expulsion

Students with an overall score less than 60% may not return to the Academy the following year. And if a student has been so expelled, they must audition again a year later for consideration. Students who have overall scores between 60% and 65% will be on Academic Probation the first quarter of the following year. At the end of that quarter, a Review Committee will be called to decide if probation can be lifted, or if the student is to be expelled for academic reasons.

Behavioral Expulsion

Students may be expelled for behavior. Behavior Expulsion is irreversible. Vandalism, theft, conviction of civil crimes, indecent exposure, lewd behavior, alcohol or drug possession at the Academy or during an Academy sponsored function (trip, performance, meeting, press conference, etc.), and inflicting injury to a fellow student, faculty or staff member, are all reasons for instantaneous behavioral expulsion.

Dance Competitions

In addition, there are a few other occasions that will result in Behavioral Expulsion. Students who are not permitted to start working on pointe and are found to be doing so elsewhere will be expelled. Students participating in public performances that have not been approved in writing by the Academy will be expelled. Students participating in competition without being directly sponsored at the event by the Academy will be expelled. Students selling Academy property, photos, recordings, video/film, and other materials will be expelled.

Adjudication by Review Committee

In addition, when necessary due to actions deemed inappropriate by the Academy, a Review Committee will be formed to judge if said behavior is to be dealt with by Behavioral Expulsion, Academic Probation, penalty or punitive actions.

Academy Traditions

Though ballet is a relatively young art form, it has 450 years of history. Throughout that history, each national ballet style (French, Italian, Russian, English, American) has established its own traditions. Many of these are similar to each other, as would be expected since they reflect the same art form, with the same demands. When Dame Margot and Ken Ludden were formulating the plan for the Academy that would have her name, she felt that returning to the very origins of ballet was the most appropriate. And so, at the Margot Fonteyn Academy of Ballet, we have instituted basic traditions that reflect the French origin of classical theatrical dancing in its very first historic form.

Formation of an Artist

The ultimate job of a dancer, as with any artist, is to make a personal statement of expression to an audience. To do this the ballet dancer must be trained to stand independently in their expression, and to have a training that is very carefully crafted for the specific individual, beginning when they are a child.

Far before students start actually training the body's muscles, children begin their education by being trained to express themselves through movement. This is in the form of Creative Movement and Pre-Ballet classes offered to children too young to enter the Academy, but who show promise and interest in the art form. Though not requisite for entry into the Academy, children who complete these two years of study are ready to begin their development toward the goal of becoming artists.

For expression to have artistic value it must have several elements. First it must be purely honest expression, which gives it authenticity. This is a process that begins from the very first time a child enters the studio. They and their classmates are an organic entity meeting the instructor. This entity needs to find its form, order, identity, social relationships, natural laws, assets and limitations. Each thing that occurs is taken in by the instructor and used.

Any influence from the world outside of classical ballet detracts from the task at hand, and particularly in the first couple of years will have a permanent impact from a temporary source. This will then unbalance the individuals in that group for the rest of their careers. Like poor nutrition in pregnancy, or smoking or drinking during gestation, these external influences alter the chemical, biological and physical structure of the fetus forever, and with each passing year the impact branches further out until the result is all together different than what nature intended.

In terms of Academy training, we seek to keep the atmosphere within the classrooms and studios pure of the outside influences that may permanently alter the future development of the students. Yet there are things that happen beyond the control of the Academy (a leak in the roof, an electrical short, a car accident out front one day, etc., are things that have happened in the past three years here and have a lasting impact). While it is impossible to avoid all outside elements, we do try to deliver the purest atmosphere possible.

Second, the expression must come wholly from within. This means that the artist needs to learn to be completely him- or herself. Commercial dancing (Broadway, jazz, tap, hip-hop, crumping, etc.) responds to audience desires and demands. These demands, and the requirement of commercial enterprises to maximize profits, determine the content, pace, development and purposes of such performances. Dance schools are commercial enterprises, designed to make money, and they teach the students to please the audience, to satisfy the desires of those around them.

Our world is very different. The fine art of classical theatrical dancing is in the realm of philosophers, master painters, composers and virtuoso musical interpreters. These artists lead the world, not pander to it. Audiences come to see fine art to be inspired, taken to a new place, expanded, challenged, shown a new way of viewing that is foreign or unfamiliar to them.

An Academy prepares artists to know themselves completely, without any of the kind of emotional or psychological pull that would come from being in front of family, friends or public. Children are automatically eager to please, and will alter everything about what they do if anyone from outside of the Academy and its world is present in the classroom. Parents will see, however, that when their children come out of the room they often rush to show you what they've learned. Compared to everything that is done in the class, what the students choose to show to their parents and friends is the result of them having learned, explored, invented or perfected something from the work they've done that they then can show to you as their own accomplishment. Being away allows them to find their voice, develop their skill, and then lead their audience with their own personal expression of that learning. It is their very first experience as an artist. Having parents or friends in the room makes this impossible, and changes the atmosphere so much that even what ends up being learned changes.

Third, the technique used in expression must always be fully within the grasp of the artist. Learning technique is very hard. Developing the means to cope with failed attempts, a success that defies recreation a second time, understanding that something must be done over and over to even begin to feel natural, and at the same time each student must be led to find the willingness to try the new, knowing first attempts will not be successful and should not be.

When students feel the compulsion to impress, or are embarrassed over the need to perform something new and unfamiliar, they have an added pressure to get it right as they try to get it started. Unless they discover that there is nowhere to turn but one's inner self in order to find the resources needed, then they cannot learn anything. Instead, they will be constantly faking the "look" of a thing to please rather than doing it in front of the teacher.

All of the teachers at our Academy know when to encourage, what to encourage, when to correct, what to ignore, what to demand, etc. The emerging artist needs these wise eyes alone, just as they need to develop a relationship with the fact one always needs an informed, sophisticated, talented professional's eyes to see what is impossible to see from inside while trying to dance. The vast majority of the professional dancers and retired professional dancers are not viewed as qualified by this institution to take such a role with the children. The end result of an Academy education must meet a particular standard, or it is meaningless.

Fourth, the connection with the audience must be done in such a way that the artist is primary, and audience is secondary in terms of the content, pace and delivery. Confidence has an arrogance to it by its very nature, because the kind of confidence a serious artist has exists with or without an audience, with or without favorable reviews, with or without applause. It is a cold, steady, assured, poised, elegant, efficient and simple thing.

A young child approaching the possibility of finding and nurturing their internal gifts into a formidable career must have this confidence instilled in them. This does not come from praise alone, though that is an important part of it. But it is being given the knowledge to know, without any doubt, when something is authentic, hits its mark, and truly expresses what is within their heart and soul to express.

This first involves being viewed solely by their instructor in their developmental process and then, based on what the instructor sees and senses, being guided to grasp the nuances of it internally so that the ultimate praise comes from inside, that the thing that needed to get out has gotten out. Even for young children this is an amazingly complex process. For by the time they are 4 they have already been imprinted with all of the challenges they will encounter from within. By then they have learned their basic prejudices, their basic moral code, their basic world view and their basic internal code of conduct.

They must be shown how to get through and beneath all of these layers and express that which must be expressed without any of the filters society has put in the way to warp that expression. First successful attempts come easily and naturally, but are mixed in with many false starts, successes in imitating others, or close but not perfect attempts. Each child must come face to face with who they are, and this means that sometimes there is bad behavior, or an inability to express through an inhibition, or sudden unexpected anger. The instructor watches for these moments, and when they appear must deal with them creatively, in a nurturing way that still holds the child to the task at hand.

Fifth, the rules of the art form must be known so well that the choice of breaking them or not depends entirely on the expression that is being made and what will best deliver that expression to that specific audience. Techniques learned must be put into practice. The young artist gradually learns who they are, what is fulfilling expression and what is merely satisfying expression, and how to go about doing the things that can express this.

Then there is the obstacle of audience presence, or the challenge of choreography. This expression must be made using the steps and ideas of the choreographer, and in a "grammar" that makes them understood by the audience. What happens here is difficult for the child, because just making the expression and using the tools well at hand to do so is suddenly not nearly enough. The job they thought they were doing so well may work in one situation and not at all in another. A movement that felt so fulfilling at one tempo can feel robotic and devoid of feeling at another tempo. It is these larger structures that they must learn to navigate. They must learn the laws of navigation, the rules of the venue, and the confines of the environment.

Writers may perfectly express themselves in French prose, only to find that having to express the same thing in English just doesn't translate at all. A master stone mason may be all thumbs when trying to sculpt the natural landscape around their carved masterpiece, which might now seem out of place. And so it is with everything in the fine art of dancing.

There are many other aspects beyond these, and with each passing level in art academy training, this complex picture is developed, analyzed, understood and the emerging artist is then led to the next level.

Viewing Classes – A Note to Parents

Each class your children go into that room and go through part of this training process. When they come out the rush to you, proud of their accomplishments they don't show you the struggle they had to learn how. They don't show you what they had to do emotionally to find that place. They don't show you the first awkward attempt at a new technique. What they show you is what they feel good about, what excites them and what they are confident in. For them to have had that pure space in which they had complete internal and external freedom to learn, then allows them to show you, the person they love so much, the results rather than the process.

Often when parents stop in to view "progress" they will misunderstand the relative importance of what they view. They may hear the instructor give a correction and have no idea what the larger context is for that correction. Consequently, a parent or friend may praise something that should not be praised, and withhold praise on something that desperately needs it. And surprisingly, it often has very little to do with how something "looks", whether it is executed well or not.

And so, at a dance school everything is for the audience, for the parents, and for ultimate profit. In an Academy, the audience and family must wait until there is something the young artist elects to show. And remember that these introductory sessions are more impactful than later lessons. A skew in trajectory here will offset an entire career. Parents will get to see the results each day to the extent to which the student decides to share it, but no outsider sees the process.

Once students are old enough and developed enough to be in the Academy, then they must perform, which is the ultimate result of all of the training. But performance means that something is learned, practiced, refined and prepared before hand. The performance opportunities the students have are the Défilé and Grand Défilé each year at which they present their work. And while students will have many assignments along the way they may choose to share with others, the public will have to wait for the finished products. In the meantime, be pleased with the little performances students choose to give after they are finished with daily classes along the way.

Défilé

Our Défilé, which is held each year about two months after the school year starts, is a direct link to the origins of ballet's very first days. King Louis XIV was fond of dancing, and was particularly impressed with fancy footwork. To develop a dance form he turned to his fencing master, as fencing provided a basic set of foot positions that blend maximum stability with maximum ability to move quickly. What's more, in those days, fencing in one form or another was the means by which people defended themselves, and so knowledge of these basic positions and movements was as prevalent then as knowledge of how to use passwords for computer security is today.

King Louis bade his sentries scour the kingdom for anyone with supple body, shapely ankles, and inventive footwork. These gifted folk were brought to the King's monthly ball and participated in a parade (or *défilé* in French), during which all of the gathered subjects with dance steps to show the King came forward one at a time to present their dance step to the King.

Following this tradition, the Academy has a Défilé at the beginning of each school year. At the Défilé a legendary ballerina sits in the studio and the students present themselves to her. They perform simple classroom steps for her, showing their level at the time. In addition, each student presents a short oral biography of one of the icons of dance history to the ballerina, and also speaks extemporaneously about films they've researched of that person's work and/or legacy. The ensuing short conversation between new student and ballerina forms the first direct link in the young dancer's life to their predecessors.

At the end of these exchanges, the ballerina teaches the students about some aspect of ballet (classical mime, costume history, trends in the ballet, etc.). At the end of the day there is a reception for students, parents and the ballerina.

In our first three years, Joy Williams Brown (lifelong friend of Fonteyn's, and President, in America, of the Royal Academy of Dance for more than 40 years, earning her the title "voice of Fonteyn") has greeted the new students. In preparing an exhibit called "Fonteyn in America" for the Lincoln Center Library, Brown discovered some previously unknown photographs of Margot Fonteyn demonstrating the various classical pantomime positions. In our Défilé, she has displayed these rare photographs, and given a lecture on classical pantomime to the students.

Grand Défilé

In the time of King Louis XIV, ability to dance and being clever with steps was one of the very few ways a person of low birth might enter the Royal court. At each ball, during the Défilé for King Louis, some of the peasants would be chosen to join the Royal dance. At the end of the social season, then, those who had most pleased the King were asked to participate in the Grand Défilé, where they would show their most favored steps, and dance in the large demonstration dances for the evening's primary entertainment. It was during these that the King might invite someone into his court.

At the Academy our Grand Défilé serves as our end-of-year graded performance for the students. Every point of contact with the public is graded by an Examiners Panel, consisting of five top professionals in their fields of performing arts.

In the Lower School, the evening consists of an original piece conceived, choreographed and performed by each student. These short pieces are movement studies, and are no longer than two minutes. All Lower School students must present such a work. In addition, then, Level 3 and 4 students must also perform assigned variations, on pointe for the girls. This is their first experience with classical choreography, which has been simplified so they are able to reasonably master it for performance. They must research, design and render their costumes for everything performed on that evening, and they prepare their own program notes, including a personal biography.

Upper School students, on a different evening, perform actual classical repertoire, and have been coached in their roles. They also perform in a larger work all together, embracing another old tradition, this time from Germany (see *Geburts Musikschule* section). This Grand Défilé is much more like a professional performance, and tickets to it are sold to the public.

Geburts Musikschule Performances

A group of composers in the early 20th Century, led by Carl Orff, set about to correct a basic flaw in the way individuals in western civilization are introduced to music. They noticed that all of the folk songs and children's songs were very simplistic musical constructions. And when those children grow up and are faced with symphonic music, they are utterly lost and find the music challenging at best, and displeasing at worst. And so they set about to revamp the way music was presented to the general population, and taught to musical artists. The beautiful and haunting folk songs of Bela Bartok are part of the grand legacy of this movement, and the presence of popular symphonies of Romeo and Juliet, Cinderella and Peter and the Wolf are also thanks to this same movement. But beyond these rare examples, the audience became estranged from the fare of the concert hall, and turned to pop music, or sugar-coated and insipid renditions of classical themes played in public places.

The teaching of music was another problem, for even top conservatory students were beginning to be limited in t heir ability to interpret classical and symphonic masterworks. They noticed that the conservatory student was put to the task of presenting recitals consisting of serious music that takes virtuosity to master the technique of these pieces, and so the interpretive artistry was left by the wayside. A generation of competent technical performers who could play very difficult music, but couldn't express any emotion at all in their music came to the fore, and audiences gradually lost complete touch with symphony orchestras, operas and the like.

And so they set about to create a series of works for various levels of students. Works that were written to accommodate the technical level of the students, while by design demanding some sort of interpretation. These works, taking their lead from the popular Stravinsky/Ramus collaboration "L'Histoire d'un Soldat", involve orchestra, chorus, singers, dancers and actors. Each work has a plot twist that can go any number of ways, and alternate endings are written. It is up to the performers themselves, on stage and during a live performance, to use their interpretation to shift the course of that performance to land in one of the endings.

An example might be helpful. One of the works is called "Der Ja-sager, Der Nein-sager" ("The Yea-sayer, the Nay-sayer"). The work takes place in a coastal Japanese village. The protagonist learns that a Tsunami is approaching in a matter of hours, and if the inhabitants of the village do not ascent the surrounding mountains, they will all die. He calls the entire town together and explains the situation. He points out that every person in the village is part of what makes their community, and he urges them to agree that nobody will be left behind—that the community will survive intact. And so, this agreed, they commence their climb up the mountain.

Very soon after, the leader himself falls and breaks his legs. He cannot go forward, and urges them to leave him and save themselves. One of the members of the village reminds the rest of their initial agreement, and refuses to go on unless they find a way of bringing the injured man along. And so the fixed part of the plot sits. From that point forward each character has options as to what they will sing, dance or act. And so the ensemble must, by the power of their interpretations, bring the work to a conclusion. All of the music, text and choreography is such that students of those art forms can master the techniques, and so it rests on each of them to find the power of their interpretation to shape the outcome. There are many of these productions.

In the Academy's Upper School, each year one of these productions, or a new work in this vein, is presented as the finale of the evening. And, of course, everything is graded by a panel of 5 members.

Colin Milnes Award

In the second year of the Academy, Colin Milnes became the president of the National Arts Group Board of Directors. He facilitated the formation of Swiss and British societies to support the Academy, and helped with the production of the Nutcracker. He also managed a tour of the US and Europe of Ludden's newest work at that time "The Wind's Bride". In the Spring of 2009 he was moving to New York to facilitate the Grand Défilé, then was going to become the General Manager of the Academy.

In a shocking and swift chain of events, he became ill over the Christmas holidays, and died just one week after he was diagnosed with cancer. He was so devoted to the Academy, that his family has created the Colin Milnes Award, to be given to the top student of the Academy each year, decided at the Grand Défilé. And so, on May 17, 2009, the first two Colin Milnes Awards were given. As there was only a Lower School at that time, the awards were given to Alexander Bushkin as the top student in the Grand Défilé 2008, and Brianna Rivera as the top student in 2009. The award is given each year.

My Song

The General Arts Curriculum features a course called "Natures". The course is designed to help students understand their own nature, and then to express it outwardly.

The course is split into two parts, Natures I: Identity Project (which starts each school year), and Natures II: My Song (which ends each year). In Natures I: Identity Project, each student makes a visual arts 'passport'. It is a notebook of sketches and drawings such that if another person looks at the art works, they will understand the identity of the student.

Natures II: My Song consists of a song each student writes. They must compose the music, write the lyrics, arrange the song, and prepare it for public performance. The Academy engages a professional singer/songwriter to work with the students each year, and then, at the Grand Défilé, to perform the works. In 2009, Chuck E. Costa recorded all of the songs, which are available as a CD through the Academy, or via iTunes on the Internet. Each year another CD is produced of the songs.

Nutcracker Ballet

Les Ballets du Monde, the professional performing ballet company of the National Arts Group, is a company of top dancers from around the world who come together to perform various works. The performances have been ongoing since 1978, and Ballets du Monde is affiliated through National Arts Group with the Academy.

Many years they put on a production of the Nutcracker Ballet in which Academy students perform. Lower School students perform as children in Act I and as mice and soldiers in Act II; Upper School students are the corps de ballet for the Snow and Waltz of the Flowers numbers, and take various roles throughout the production.

This gives Academy students exposure to professional dancers, performance experience in a professional theater with a professional production, and brings their dancing to the attention of the general public and critical press from their earliest years.

Academy Programs

Dame Fonteyn designed an educational system that she thought would best prepare classical dance professionals for solid careers in their dancing years, and the skills to continue working in the field of classical ballet beyond their stage career. Originally, the programs were only in music, drama and painting. But as development of the concept for the Academy progressed, it became clear the value of studying the history of these art forms, as well as other more scholarly subjects. She came to this conclusion while preparing the "Magic of Dance" series, learning firsthand how important understanding the societal and cultural context of any moment in art. The result was a very substantial television series and book, as well as the addition of the Scholarly Arts Program to her plan for the Academy.

Scholarly Arts Program

The Scholarly Arts division provides education in the General Arts Studies. It covers areas such as Art History, Music History, Gallery Curation, Criticism/Review, and other scholarly areas that are part of the overall picture of a career in the performing arts.

Field trips to museums are included in this portion of the educational program, along with guest lectures and various special events. As history is made in relation to the arts, these discoveries, excavations, inventions or innovations are thoroughly discussed.

Musical Arts Program

Music is the life blood of the dance. Until very recently in the history of theatrically presented dance, music has always been the foundation. Many famous composers have contributed to the considerable body of works that have been choreographed. And even in works without a composed or improvised musical score, rhythm and pulse are nearly always underlying foundational elements to dance. Hence, the understanding of music is an essential foundation of classical ballet. The Musical Arts Department of the Academy, oversees the musical education of students from their first entry into the Academy, through their eventual graduation. They begin with classes in musical awareness, the history and appreciation of music, and proceed to learn to read music, understand the basic principles of musical theory, etc.

Studio Arts Program

Studio Arts encompass drawing, sculpture, painting, composition, costuming, stage settings, graphic arts and design. A dancer is a living paintbrush in the hands of the choreographer, and the stage is the three dimensional canvas of the proscenium stage. The more a dancer understands the whole design and impact of the picture in which s/he dances, the more effective will be their artistic decisions of how to best interpret the part they are dancing. Students at the academy begin with basic courses in sculpture (to begin to understand the interplay between positive and negative space), and go on to develop skills in drawing, design, costuming, stage set construction, etc.

Dramatic Arts Program

Dramatic arts study is critical for the classical dancer. Students begin to study drama in their first year, with basic acting skills. As they progress through the Academy, they eventually receive broad scoped training in acting, stage combat, dramatic reading, film acting, and many more subjects.

Specialty Classes

In addition to ballet technique classes, specialty classes will be offered and required for students. Specialty Classes include – classical variations, classical partnering, contemporary variations, contemporary partnering, character dancing, acting for dance, pantomime, romantic style, classic style, bravura style, neo-classic style, International Dance, traditional tribal dance, Balanchine style, Graham Technique, Hawkins Technique, and Alexander Technique. Specialty classes will be specifically required at different times in the student's Academy career. This will be partially determined by availability, and partially by the student's level of ability. As they take these classes, they will then pass a classroom exam so that they receive credit for having successfully completed that study. These credits will be considered when a student is seeking to enter the Upper School.

Such technical specialties as pointe or men's classes will be offered as regular technique classes and are required of all students all the time once they have reached that level of physical ability. There will be separate audition classes in pointe technique and men's dance technique for entry into the Upper School

MFAB Educational Program

Overview

The educational vision of Margot Fonteyn is innovative, elegant, and absolutely sensible. Her basic philosophy that ballet dancers will achieve their greatest artistic fulfillment when they have studied, in depth, the various art forms that come together to make up classical ballet is impossible to find fault with it is so logical.

The ultimate challenge is more than just teaching the various art forms to students of ballet, which is a simple thing to do given the resources and opportunity, but it is bringing those various aspects of the art form together into a fully integrated whole. The curriculum at MFAB is designed to do just that.

The muscles must be carefully trained, in the correct order. This is to ensure that each child develops the exact combination of strength, stretch, coordination and rhythm so that they are able to achieve the various steps. Ballet is difficult, and therefore can seem defeating to a young student if they try to do a technical movement before they are ready. When children are pushed too quickly ahead, they will suffer injuries in the short term, and debilitating ailments later in life. Too much stress can create deformities as the bones grow; too much stretch can weaken joints and cause secondary injuries.

A similar sequence is necessary when developing the other art forms, and giving assignments that demand bringing the different arts together in a harmonious unity. And so Fonteyn and Ludden, in consultation with accomplished artists in the various related art forms, created the sequence of subjects, the assignments and examinations that would be appropriate to each level of ability, and the basic methods for approaching the young artist at various stages of development. And the age of entry into the Academy is designed with this in mind.

In the theater, as in most endeavors in life, a person cannot get far by doing the minimum. And it is those who go beyond the minimum, bringing in everything they can, who achieve the most in the arts. To reinforce this, extra credit is given for everything a student does over and above any assignment or test question. This also establishes the essential truth that when performing or creating art the artist is speaking to his or her audience, and leading them with their expression and innovation. By seeking to show off their understanding of related, peripheral concepts, and to find ways to express through coordinating different elements to make a whole greater than the sum of its parts, the student is by definition finding their own unique voice, and expressing what they, as an individual artist, have to offer.

Etiquette is also paramount in the world of classical ballet. A ballet performance is a huge organism of interrelated, but extremely different, parts. Each person must do their part to their fullest, but also be aware of what all of the others around them are also doing. Indeed, the most important person in that group is often not present at a ballet performance, as the choreographer and the composer of the music are rarely present. The kind of mutual respect needed between people sharing a dressing room, an entrance way to the stage or a mirror is obvious. But it is the integrity of the dancer to respect the choreographer, and be a true embodiment of the music that has no overseer, other than a conscientious director or regisseure. The basic rules of etiquette are required from the first experience of the audition, and the more sophisticated and complex social etiquette within the classroom, rehearsal hall and on stage are required and visibly corrected in front of all gathered when transgressed, so that everyone present knows at all times that each one is to be held to the established standard of conduct.

School Levels

The Academy is divided into two schools, the Lower School and the Upper School. The basic division between them is that in the Lower School, students learn how to execute steps in ballet, read and write music, approach the basic techniques of dramatic presentation, and master elemental techniques of design, drawing, color, composition and statements in visual arts. In the Upper School, the emphasis is on refining techniques, and approaching the expression of statements through these techniques.

Lower School Structure

The Lower School is divided into four levels, numbered sequentially. Each level has a specific goal in the development of the facility of the student (mind, body, psychology and emotions), and the technique of performing the various elements of each art form.

It is assumed that students will spend a minimum of two years at each level in the Lower School, thus taking an expected minimum of 8 years to graduate.

Level 1 Studies

Level 1 introduces students to the basics they will need throughout their time at MFAB, and lays a solid foundation for their future careers as professionals in performing arts. In line with MFAB's commitment to the whole dancer's whole life, the basic skills in this level are designed to shape the entire life experience and point of view of the person, not just the artist. Creative enterprises are based on a balance between both sides of the brain, and a fluid interaction between them.

In this level MFAB administration, staff and faculty are learning as much about the student as the student is learning about his or her future as a citizen of the world. They must learn to identify, understand and follow intricate sets of rules and requirements, while at the same time being true to their own vision and feel confident to bring their vision into the world. It is through basic skills learned in Level 1 that they will accomplish this, and so this level is perhaps the most critical level of all. Everything in their future will be built on what they learn in this level.

Ballet L1

Level 1 ballet organizes the body for ballet, and teaches the basic ambulatory steps. In this level the students master the arm and leg positions, the basic linear exercises at the barre, the first four porte de bras exercises, and the twelve most basic ways of moving forward, backward, upward, downward, and around.

In their introductory classes they are taught how to achieve a dancing posture in the body, maximum but 'honest' turnout, and the complex coordination required to properly point the foot. They are also taught the directional orientation grid for proscenium performance, and the proper pitch and focus of the shoulders, neck and head.

They keep notebooks of all ballet terms, and are periodically asked to write down the names of the exercises, positions, steps and movements. They are encouraged to use correct spelling by the fact that they receive extra credit for correct spelling and punctuation in French, but it does not count against their scores if a word is misspelled, when the attempt is clear to express the correct answer.

The dual truths of ballet— "the music is never wrong" and "the step is never wrong"— are drilled from the first. At the same time, students are reminded that in the ballet class they are to pay attention to their own dancing, not to themselves or to the dancing of others. These simple lessons set the ground rules for ballet etiquette, and appropriate application of one's energies.

Music L1

Students must learn to read from middle-C to high-C on the treble clef, as well as the dynamics and incidentals of musical notation. They have in depth study of rhythm, and must be at home with time signatures and musical accents.

Students write rhythmic compositions for each other to play or perform. And they are also required to use found objects as musical instruments, eking from them their full range of sound capability. When their composition is performed or played by others, they must conduct it, making routine, visible and clear movements to denote the various beats. To do this they are taught basic standard means of conducting with a baton or just with their hands and fingers.

At the same time, listening to and enjoying music is reinforced at every opportunity. As a dancer one must embody the music, not dance to it. Therefore, music is taught as part of the body through clapping, stomping, making audible noises with the voice and using every surface as if it is a musical instrument.

Drama L1

Students explore development of characters in physical and improvisational terms. They are given a variety of assignments designed to take what they think of as play and begin to assign specific parameters to it. Emphasis is on creating a unique characterization that does indeed portray that which is intended. This is achieved through constructive critique, analysis of character-unique elements, and seeing how and if predetermined objectives for the character are achieved.

They also construct simple plots for a collection of characters and then use guided or structured improvisation to act out the plot. They are urged to observe life around them for ideas, as well as shown different videos that achieve iconic figures and standard archetypical characters.

Art L1

Level 1 art begins with drawing during their Natures I course work. At the beginning of the year, during this first exercise, they are given a sketchbook to use as a sketch diary for the year. These diaries are periodically collected and reviewed, and at the end of each year the sketch diary is added to the student's file.

In Level 1 Art the students are introduced to clay sculpture. They first use non-drying, oil-based clay and learn the coil construction technique. After this is accomplished they then build a "crazy box" which is a free-form box that is shaped based on how the lumps of clay roll out, and then decorated.

After they have done these two with oil-based clay, they then make a project of their choice with clay that is baked.

Scholarly Studies L1

All students take 'Natures 1 – Identity Project' and 'Natures 2 – My Song' each year they are in MFAB. Each year at the Défilé each student studies the history of one of the legendary ballet icons that are built into the back-board of the barre in their studio.

Level 1 students study some of the stories of ancient mythology and learn about archetypes, with exercises so they can relate these archetypes to people they know in their own world. Level 1 students also study health and hygiene as two separate courses. These studies are not specifically related to the study of dance, however, but just as information on how the body works in general.

Level 2 Studies

Overall emphasis for Level 2 students is on style and line. In ballet these two are quite obvious, and equally obvious is how they work together for the visual impact of the dancer. By Level 2 the students are at a point in their development (ages 10-12) that introduces becoming aware of how one looks to others and to the outside world. By teaching principles of style and line across the boards, the students learn how poise, presentation and harmony of behavior to the surroundings can help to make the impact desired on others.

They also become aware that they must be the ambassador for classical ballet to their families and pier groups, for the demands are such that they will have lives quite different from the norm. Again, this is all about interaction with outside viewers, and to develop a sense of style and line helps a great deal in establishing confidence and grace.

Ballet L2

Having mastered body positions, directions, and means of moving across the floor or into the air in Level 1, their muscles are now ready for more strenuous demands to be made on them, and to stretch. In Level 2, therefore, controlling movement, or maintaining the body position while that position is moving (i.e., grand jeté, promenade, pirouettes, etc.) is introduced. At the same time, students must master porte de bras exercises 5 through 7.

Also at this level are more complex patterns of moving across the floor ('diamond step') or through the air (sauté fuetté). In keeping with emphasis on line they begin to learn much more sophisticated stretches, done in a far more demanding daily routine, and they are required to master épaulement. The 9 body attitudes are introduced only in pointe tendue positions and must be thoroughly mastered to graduate and move on.

As girls approach their second year of this level they are introduced to pointe if they are ready muscularly, skeletally and of proper age. Male students begin to take men's class with Level 2 and will continue to do so throughout the rest of their lives as dancers. And last year students of Level 2 must perform an assigned piece of choreography at the Grand Défilé as well as their own work.

Music L2

Here the bass clef is added to their ability to read and write music, from middle-C to low-C only. Along with this they learn basic compositional forms (Sonata-Allegro and Passacaglia) and are asked to recognize elements of these compositional forms in the music in their own lives.

The focus on the musical line and musical style are brought to their focus, and they are asked to write small compositions that would best express an assigned mood. In their My Song compositions they must provide the melody line throughout, and where possible a bass line simultaneously, though without formal learning about chord structure. This helps them develop their ear to hear harmonies, leading tones, and how note combinations reflect or establish mood.

Level 2 students are encouraged to study a single voiced instrument (recorder, flute, clarinet, voice, etc.) so that they can expand their knowledge of music and refine their ability to read music.

Drama L2

Students now start to break down scenes from a script, and answer the standard 3 questions for every character in a scene. They learn to write plays, and must write, rehearse and perform plays as a group, or in small groups.

With their individual characterizations in class, in MFAB traditional performances and if they are onstage with

Les Ballets du Monde, they are graded for characterization, character development and establishing mood.

Art L2

Level 2 brings two sculpture classes. The first is a study of negative and positive space. They study the sculptural photographs of Max Waldman, Primitive Art, modern works and their own bodies in ballet positions.

The second study is building a shape on a hard wire armature. They must, however, begin with a sketch or scribble and then turn it into a three dimensional, free-standing form. And in their Identity Project works they must now introduce the blending of color with mood, shape, content and desired impact on the viewer.

Scholarly Arts L2

All students take 'Natures 1 – Identity Project' and 'Natures 2 – My Song' each year they are in MFAB. Each year at the Défilé each student studies the history of one of the legendary ballet icons that are built into the back-board of the barre in their studio.

Students here learn fencing to better understand the origins of classical ballet, but also to understand how turnout equals stability in motion and when suddenly thrust into an out of balance pose. They also study Ballet Basics, after which they are required to sew all of their own shoes, maintain their own ballet class wardrobe and do their own hair. They also take two different classes in Stage Make-Up. In the first they study the principles and procedures of basic stage make-up, with a bent toward creating original characters. The second Stage Make-up course teaches how to embellish your own face for stage, how to create the effect of aging. In this course they learn techniques for using crèpe hair and building facial prosthetics.

Cyclical evolution of style throughout the history of art is taught. The seemingly organic movement from realism, to mannerism, to surrealism, to abstraction is studied and then applied to the student's own lifetime of images surrounding them in the world.

Level 3 Studies

By Level 3 it is time to start to connect the dots. Students have learned basic techniques, and the presentation to the audience. Their muscles are now developing, both due to their physical maturity and the amount of training they've had thus far, and so they are able to combine different areas of their technical skills and imaginations to make statements.

But their statements must have depth, and their presentations to the public must cause a reaction, provoke a thought, or instigate action on the part of those watching. This can be in the form of making someone laugh or cry, giving inspiration that compels some sort of action or discussion, cause discomfort from examination of conscious, or many other impacting states. As teenagers now they want independence, but they must use that independence to deliver something to the world around them, or extract something from it. Artists are visionaries; they are the leaders of hearts and minds, rather than bodies. They must find their rhythm.

Level 3 shows us our first glimpse of what sort of artist each student may become. Their body type is now set, and their musculature, and control of it for intended purpose, is now bringing evidence of a personal stamp—the artistic identity.

Ballet L3

The body is now formed enough that it is possible to introduce many things. Girls are en pointe, boys are starting to learn their male virtuosity steps, batterie is introduced, and internal rhythm in turns, beats, preparatory phrases and more.

Limits are pushed and expanded, and it is no longer acceptable to simply jump, but it is now important the shape of the arch in the air that the jump takes, or how exactly it fits into the musical phrase. The students must now master all nine of the standard porte de bras exercises, perform all nine body attitudes using a wide variety of steps, and start to learn some of the basic fixed adagios.

They must master the three basic types of pirouettes (adagio, allegro, and tire bouchon), and be able to properly select which type of pirouette is called for in different combinations. They must also be able to clearly demonstrate the difference in execution between élevé, enlevé and rélevé.

Stretching is now a way of life, as are all things ballet. The demands are intensified, but so is the expressiveness and the joy.

Music L3

At Level 3 students are encouraged to start learning a harmonic instrument (guitar, piano, xylophone, etc.) or to sing choral music with a school group. They are also asked frequently to find elements of music in conductor's scores of ballets and operas, which MFAB has in its Boniello Library, or from the individual song reductions in the Sarria Collection of that library.

The central focus of the study of music at this level is the study of intervals in the Western scale, triad formations, and the relative major and minor keys to various scales. They must write a paper on some aspect of triad formation in popular music as well.

They join together with Level 1 and Level 2 students by working with them on their My Song entries, flushing out the harmonic setting of the melodies the younger students have already written.

In addition, Level 3 students must write all of their entries for My Song—lyrics, melody, bass line, harmonies and include in the final written song dynamic markings and proper incidentals. Throughout this study they are introduced to the way music theory works, but are not required to master basic music theory at this time, just intervals in the Western scale, triads and relative keys.

Drama L3

Level 3 students now have actual acting class, and must prepare monologues and scenes. They hold mock auditions in front of music faculty and guest artists, at which they are required to prepare three monologues—a tragedy, a romantic piece and a comedic piece—which they perform for a grade in front of the class.

They critique each others' work, and must write a monologue. This monologue is then prepared by another student under the direction of its author and the drama teacher.

For their Grand Défilé original work they may select to act a scene or perform a monologue instead of creating a movement piece, though they are encouraged, if opting to demonstrate original acting ability, to incorporate as much of music and dance as they can.

Art L3

Students take a double-long course in design, learning design techniques with pencil, marker pens, pen and ink, and *gouache* (or water color). They must create a color wheel of four levels, and must complete a project that incorporates the elements of design they've learned.

In their art studies, they must create a 'Light Box' as a half-year project. This is a *papier machée* box painted white with Gesso, and then covered with a thin layer of colored tissue paper that has had a design drawn onto it with colored pencil. The box must show a related series of images in some sort of stepped-developmental process on the exterior and interior walls.

Scholarly Arts L3

All students take 'Natures 1 – Identity Project' and 'Natures 2 – My Song' each year they are in MFAB. Each year at the Défilé each student studies the history of one of the legendary ballet icons that are built into the back-board of the barre in their studio.

Level 3 students study basic Anatomy for dance with a detailed analysis of one exercise from their barre work written and presented to the class.

They study dance history and must create a Ballet Time-Line that is then on display in the Academy for the remainder of the year.

In their second year of Level 3 they are required to attend the 'Salon', a weekly discussion of the history of art, with periodic presentations and papers due throughout the year. In this course they are graded on participation, contribution, evidence of outside study, attendance and their ability to join into group discussions with a vital point of view, and the ability to explain and even defend this point of view.

They also study the history of dance costumes and hand in a written critique of the costumes designed for the Grand Défilé.

Level 4 Studies

The final level of the Lower School brings the entire dancer together as an artist. Developmental phrasing, artistic expression, clear point of view and intentional interpretation are all emphasized in the various aspects of their work. They have some year-long projects, and take on a mentorship role to younger fellow students in the Lower School.

At the same time they start to address some of the larger issues, beyond what is presented on stage or in the gallery, related to public showings of art forms.

Ballet L4

At this level, dancers must be able to create an interpretation that carries through the many phrases in a piece of choreography. Their bodies are now fully formed, and their technique is a strong foundation. They begin to explore *petite allegro, grande allegro, enchainements batteries*, etc.

They must have mastered derivative steps (*sissone fermé/ouvert, assemblé de vole, grand jeté en tournant, tour jeté,* etc.), and achieved the advanced steps in their basic forms.

In the center floor they must be able to execute a group of fixed adagios and allegros, and execute the bravura, classical, romantic, neo-classic, and modern lines and ways of doing steps with no cross-over of these variations of basic ballet steps into the academic, elemental version of each step.

Girls must achieve *adagio, allegro, manège, grand allegro* and *petit allegro* steps *en pointe*, and the basic coda steps as well. Boys must be able to execute all of the basic male steps of the ballet, and the full spectrum of *demi charactèr* steps as well.

Music L4

In Level 4, music is used throughout a variety of projects. On its own, the history of music is studied in terms of the development of theory and modes of expression. Conductors' scores are used to establish the basic theoretical analysis of a piece of music, and then the devices used for specific mood and expression are exposed.

In learning about music theory, students also study chord charts and sheet music from popular, secular and sacred music. By charting the simultaneous development of musical styles through the evolution of theory and device to create setting, mood and statement, the student begins to develop a strong sense of the musical mood, setting and environment they must embody when dancing.

Drama L4

The Dramatic Arts teachers are involved in coaching students for all of the works they will perform at Level 4. For each piece assigned or created, the dancers will have to do an analysis of the character being portrayed, character back story and history, physical/movement attribute of that character, and all of the fine points of acting as apply to their every moment on stage.

In their multi-media work they will be required to include dramatic passages (with or without dance movement) and be judged on clarity, placement, dramatic arch, characterization, character growth, etc.

Art L4

Level 4 students study color theory, and then apply it to their multi-media work, and/or their final project. They must apply aspects of design and composition to the editing they study, and in the many different short pieces they will have to produce.

They will also do line sketches, quick studies, and impromptu works. They apply their knowledge of anatomy, their drawing technique, their understanding of movement (both of the subject and of their own arm and hand holding the pen or pencil) and come up with a quick sketch. This also teaches them to make real what they see, how they see it, AS they see it.

Scholarly Arts L4

All students take 'Natures 1 – Identity Project' and 'Natures 2 – My Song' each year they are in MFAB. Each year at the Défilé each student studies the history of one of the legendary ballet icons that are built into the back-board of the barre in their studio.

Level 4 students are in their final years of the Lower School, and the curriculum of preparation for Upper School must be completed, rendering students of exceptional skill, talent, training, and artistic ability. In the Scholarly Arts studies at this point in their student careers delves into systems that incorporate all they've learned thus far, and puts those things together into cohesive programs ready for presentation to the public.

Students Study Pattern Drafting, Video Editing, Multi-Media Production in depth, creating many projects in their first year at Level 4. When a student is in his or her final year of the lower School, they go before a Review Committee to propose their Final Project, which will take them a full year to complete. Final Projects are full evenings of work, or full bodies of works, that are presented to the public. It may be a gallery exhibition, a film production, an evening of dance, a play, or a musical concert, if they go in a traditional direction. But a Final Project might also be a Multi-Media event, or even a public presentation that is impromptu.

All Final Projects must be approved in concept, and then in detail by the Review Panel that meets for the Spring auditions the prior school year. This gives the student the full summer to organize, do some fund raising if necessary for a project, and be prepared for the fall with a full plan developed for all aspects of their program. They are responsible not only for the content of what is performed or presented, but also must prepare the printed program, press announcements, promotional materials, posters, etc.

Final Projects are scheduled for presentation anytime from March through May of their final year, and must not conflict with the Grand Défilé.

Upper School Structure

Having acquired a firm foundation of dance technique in the Lower School, as well as a solid base of knowledge in the General Arts studies, students are now groomed for their professional careers. Their work load increases and broadens, with the gradual linking together of all of the different elements that come together in Classical Ballet, and then, in the final two tiers, they learn how to package, present, represent and advocate for their art form.

The Upper School also refines the study of arts techniques with emphasis on stylization, stylistic consistency, continuity of presentation, distillation of interpretation and effectiveness of communication through the various disciplines. In depth study of all aspects of technique is demanded. Standards are very high in the Upper School, and graduation is achieved only by those students who truly become accomplished young artists.

Apprentice Level Studies

The Apprentice Level (AL) demands that the student begin to look as technique, dramatic expression, artistic point of view, historic context, musical setting and visual impact on the stage as tools to bring into focus an overall artistic creation. Studies focus on coordination of elements, complementary and supplementary attributes of various art forms participating in the whole, and how the synergy of these art forms come together to create a unified and harmonious whole.

Ballet AL

To understand classical ballet technique and traditions, it is essential to master the wide variety of national dance forms that came together in the evolution of ballet. The national dances that are presented in classical ballets are first studied (Czardas, Hopak, Tarantella, Basque Dances, and Mazurka) and students must demonstrate proficiency in performance as well as write essays about the origins of these dances and how they reflect their indigenous cultural beginnings.

Students must also show technical proficiency and stylistic refinement of the historic dances of early European Courts (Bourrée, Gavotte, and Minuet). These historic dances are taught in form and variations, but also with acknowledgment of the subtle communication made possible between people even while in public view.

In the Grand Défilé, the variety of dances from the ballet Gayna will be performed, along with performance choreography of national dances from major classical works. These are strictly graded by specialists in these dance forms, as well as major artists from the ballet world to assure authenticity as well as the appropriate ballet context into which these dance forms must ultimately fit.

Music AL

Bringing the elements together in music involves the study of conducting. Students also study scoring, and do comparative analysis of different ways of scoring and arranging pieces of music. They are also introduced to the world of electronic music production, or reproduction, as a foundational element in their study of video production.

Drama AL

Dramatic arts studies now use developed technique and take it to a higher level. In a stage career today, having to dance a wide variety of roles, thus drawing eclecticism and variety into the needed tools every dancer must have. Dance classics have been created by Martha Graham, Kurt Joss, Jose Limon, Erik Hawkins and Paul Taylor, to name a few, and many of their inventive works were based on new types of dramatic content. At the same time, works of choreographers like Merce Cunningham, George Balanchine, and others ask dancers to have little or no dramatic purpose, using their bodies as moving sculptures rather than tools of human expression. Style Versatility is studied in drama to constantly demand new, different, unusual and innovative ways or presenting performance arts to the public.

Art AL

In the Lower School, concepts of composition, design, basic technique and overall balance have now been trained into the young artists. This is pulled together in the study of both Costuming and Stage Lighting. AL students are called on to assist Lower School students in creating their Grand Défilé works, as well as to create their own stage realities through costume, light and make-up.

Scholarly Arts AL

Art History is looked at more as an evolutionary continuum at this level. The ways that trends in art were reflected outwardly into the society of its time by impacting other arts is considered, as well as the reverse—how society affects the trends in the history of art.

Here technological advances, wars, and movements of social revolution are seen as they create great movement in the arts. The Renaissance wouldn't have happened without the preceding Bubonic plague, nor would the sexual revolution have occurred in the 1970s without the aftermath of World War II coinciding with the introduction of electronic circuitry, microscopic discovery of the world within, and space travel.

Students at this level then look at their own time, the events in current history and the build-up to geopolitical changes are presented more as a question of "what will this do to your art" than "how and why did this come about." Artists lead the world's vision, comment on its current state, and dare to dream the impossible or foresee the inevitable. Students must prepare to take in the whole and then look back at it as an artist with opportunity and obligation for that larger world.

Corps de Ballet Level Studies

This level of study focuses on working together with others to develop a unified expression that frames and supports the whole of the work being presented. In ballet it is essential to know who you fit into the overall picture, and to understand the importance of each individual dancer in terms of the audience point of view. Every dancer on stage is seen all of the time, and if the corps de ballet is unified and working as a single unit, then it frames the work presented. However, if one person varies their position, stance, arms or rhythm while dancing in unison with the others, then all that is seen is that flaw in the overall design, and the whole picture is ruined.

Ballet CBL

Corps de Ballet Level students cannot matriculate without demonstrating knowledge of the major ballets and contemporary works that incorporate a corps de ballet. These ballets include Swan Lake (acts II and IV), Giselle (Willies), Chopiniana corps, Coppelia, Graduation Ball, Nutcracker Snow Scene and Waltz of the Flowers, La Bayadere Shade Scene and the Fille Mal Gardée Festival Dance. More modern works that include this type of corps work (The Path (Sanasardo), Serenade (Balanchine), Streetcar Named Desire (Bettis), and others) will also be taught.

Student choreographic compositions at this level will focus on use of the corps de ballet for expression, to advance the plot, to establish the style and create atmospheric locale. An in depth study of similar steps and poses in stylistically differing ballets is done, and students must be able to demonstrate stylistic accuracy from ballet era to era, including contemporary styles.

Music CBL

Students at Corps de Ballet level must begin to find their own means of expression, and their own individual artistic voice. While working on issues of unification and regularity, students are introduced to Improvisation so that they can know their own vision and how it differs from that unified expression.

Choral music is examined, as well as the large sections of orchestral music that frame the overall works (strings, woodwinds, horns, etc.). With sound it is easy to hear when someone is out of tune, or on the wrong note. It is also easy to understand how the dramatic effect of a silence is destroyed when an errant note jumps wrongly out.

Another means of understanding the proper balance and unification of the whole comes in the study of the Sound Board. Students are introduced to the techniques of blending, balancing, equalizing and mastering music through this study. They can experiment with the way subtle changes effect the whole.

Drama CBL

In drama Improvisation is also studied, enabling students to adapt to changes in dramatic atmosphere and to find reserves of dramatic expression deep within themselves. In a ballet, the leads carry the dramatic development of the plot, and it is up to the other minor characters and the corps de ballet to give the appropriate setting to support the dramatic developments.

Also studied is the Greek Chorus in early plays, performing the works in class and seeing the interplay between main characters and chorus, which originally was the purpose of the corps de ballet. Through the evolution of plays into the modern era, the role of the chorus has been altered in many ways. Students learn how they fit into the work they are doing, and how they, as young composers and choreographers, can augment the developing history of performed arts.

Art CBL

Color theory is studied to enhance understanding of the effect different colors have in compositions, and how they can be used to alter a visual scene, or focus the attention of the viewer. As the overall theme of this phase of educational development is seeing how all of the parts of the whole picture work together, color theory helps dancers understand the visual dynamics costumes, scenery, and make-up all play against each other to create the magical effects of live theater.

This study of color theory is then embellished by the Stage Design courses taken. Students' skills in various art techniques by this point are quite developed, and the constant reinforcement of their creative abilities enables them to create very effective and original stage and scene designs. As they dance on stage, they are better able to truly join with the environment the dance is placed in, and also will know what part they play in the overall picture.

Scholarly Arts CBL

The study of Music History, with comparative evaluation of how new musical forms impacted the ballet, takes on a broader scope. For the history of music is the history of civilization, belief, philosophy and attitudes about life. This is complemented by study of the History of Scene Design as well. Often ballets are set in specific periods, thereby defining the type of costumes, sets and sometimes movements used. But beyond that, with the interplay between iconic allusions to antiquity, the students are able to interpret, create and perform at a much deeper level.

As they look forward to their coming careers, and in keeping with the intention to educate the dancers for their entire lives, not only the years they will be dancing, they study Promotion. Beginning with the principles of rhetoric and poetry from Aristotle, they are taught how to most effectively construct images, words, and sounds to draw in the potential audience member, and gain support for whatever aspect of ballet they intend to promote. In understanding how the parts all fit together into the whole, they must also learn how to summarize in ways that are provocative and compelling, so that their work will have a solid audience.

Demi-Soloist Level Studies

The Demi-Soloist student must now begin to refine everything about their dancing, in preparation for ultimately taking the stage alone in solos and principal roles. To do this they study refinement of coordinated efforts, for nothing weakens a work of art more than a highly refined portion that is out of synch with that which surrounds it. Nothing in ballet is done alone, and so it is fundamentally important for dancers to learn to hone their work in tandem with others.

Ballet DSL

At Demi-Soloist level, students must master dances performed in small groups. They learn dances in the classic repertoire: from Giselle are the Friend's Dance, Miseries, Peasant Pas de Deux, and the Act I pas de deux; from Swan lake are la danse des Cignettes, Pas de Trois, and the Act II duo solos; from Cinderella are the four season fairy variations; and the Coppelia Solo, Lilac Fairy, Canary Fairy, the Nutcracker Snow Pas de Deux; and many more. Top students are selected to perform Le Pas de Quatre at the Grand Défilé.

Here are the beginning lessons on dramatic interpretation, phrasing, musicality in interpretation, stylistic variants, and how to find the exact tempo for one's own body. Coaching is a large part of this process, and working with the accompanists and drama coaches. While each student's mentor has had a guiding influence in their development thus far, at this point the mentor steps in with a more active role coaching the student.

Music DSL

Music Theory explores beneath the surface of the music. Students study theory by first learning the basic relationships of notes to keys, and keys to their logical and illogical counterparts. They will learn how to reduce a score to chord charts, and now to create the chords that link mass and melody in meaningful and effective ways. The best examples of this use of theory are, of course, the creative genius of the great masters. In the study of Music Analysis the focus is on the evolutionary moments between musical eras. It is in these times when you discover how the ultimate refinement of a musical style is then defied by the innovator, or artistic rebel, so that the next era of music evolves. In particular the music of the last four hundred years is examined, for this is when ballet was established enough to go through several golden ages of its own.

Also studied is Eurhythmics, for music, like movement, is linked directly to natural phenomena. Not only do the tempi of natural things make certain musical passages more impactful (the beating heart, falling rain, the rhythm of breathing, or the building of an avalanche), but the action associated with creating the music must also come from something purely natural and inherent to nature (a bird taking flight, a cat stalking its prey, skipping a stone on a lake, etc.). Eurhythmics teach the students what makes musical interpretation universal, and therefore with will also make their own dancing have the same universality.

Drama DSL

At the Demi-Soloist level students must master the main dramatic scenes and characters from the classical repertoire. These include Madge the Witch, Lords Capulet and Montague, Ladies Capulet and Montague, Juliet's Nurse, Friar Lawrence, Giselle's Mother, the Royal figures in Giselle, Drossylmeyer, Carabosse, Catalabut, von Rothbart, Katschii and many others. They also must appear in a student production of a play that has no music or dancing in it, which might be part of a Soloist Level final project.

Art DSL

The entire art program at the demi-soloist level is centered on Set Construction. This includes all aspects of construction, including stage properties. Well known set designs as well as innovative and brand new concept designs are planned, and scale models are built. Students in this course may be called on by Soloist Level students to participate in their Graduation Thesis projects.

Scholarly Arts DSL

Taking promotion one step further, learning Grant Writing is something any artist in the western world must understand. Grant writing is just the tip of the iceberg when seeking funds through grants. Students learn how to work with RFPs (Request For Proposals), and how to organize basic information into useful boiler plate document sections. They are also taught to study and analyze the grant giving history of a foundation, develop dossiers on board members of the foundation, and find a way of stating the case for a specific program that fits into the current purview of that foundation.

At the same time, students learn the basic theories of Eastern Healing, and the ways in which overall health and preventative measures will enhance and lengthen a career.

Soloist Level Studies

The final level of study at The Margot Fonteyn Academy of Ballet's Upper School puts the finishing touches on the dancer, and demands them to become a solo artist. Having been brought up through every aspect of all of the arts that come together in classical ballet, the soloist level student is now ready to find their unique voice as an artist, pull their own interpretations from within and present them to the world. This level of study is very closely integrated with their mentor.

Ballet SL

In the final level of Academy training, students must master not only the virtuoso solos in the classical repertoire, but also develop their own interpretations of standard classical pas des deux and solos that are often called for as standalone pieces. These roles include Giselle's Peasant Pas; Bluebird; the Chopiniana-Mazurka,-Nocturne, Male Variation, and Pas de Deux; Pas d'Esclave; Le Corsair; White Swan Pas de Deux; Paquita Variations; Nutcracker Grand Pas; Dying Swan; and from Giselle the Act II Pas de Deux, Albrecht's solos, and Giselle's Act II solos.

Students may be selected by guest choreographers to take part in creation of new works. This is where the mentor puts on the final touches, chooses repertoire for the student's work at this entire level, and also selects others to coach the different roles demanded of the student. These outside coaches are those best suited to bring out the highest artistry, as decided by the mentor or school director.

General Arts Studies SL

At the beginning of the first year in the Soloist level, students must develop a concept for their Graduate Thesis. This thesis is to demonstrate the culmination of all of their training by means of a public offering entirely created by the student—from conception through promotion, through staging, through follow up with the critical press. This thesis is approved by a specially convened Review Panel, and under the guidance of the student's mentor or an artist the mentor selects.

Throughout the development of this, the General Arts studies include courses in Stage Management, Public Speaking, Dance Business, Criticism, and development and circulation of the Press Release as a tool in their artistry.

The Graduation Thesis may include students from any level of the Upper School at the discretion of the student, and also may include students from the Lower School if approved by the Academy Director and the various faculty members of the Lower School student(s) in question.

A Graduation Thesis project may be an evening of dance, a gallery exhibition, a program of orchestral or choral music, the mounting of an original work, a multi-media production, creation and release of a DVD or musical CD, a touring exhibition, or any other creation that is approved for the project. SL students can work together if the scope of the project has clear cut delineation showing each individual student's creation, and of ample scope to warrant more than one chef.

In addition, some years the Academy Upper School will produce a Geburtsmusichschule Production in which all students must appear.

General Arts Courses

Below is a partial list of courses offered in the General Arts curriculum across Lower and Upper School, and Public Ballet, programs.

Anatomy

Art History

Ballet Costumes

Basic Design

Body Mechanics

Business In Dance

Choreography

Color Theory

Composition

Costume History

Costuming

Criticism, Review

Curation

Dance History

Drama	Public Speaking
Eastern Healing	Script Writing
Eurhythmics	Sculpture
Health	Set Building
Improvisation	Set Design
Make-Up	Song Writing
Music Analysis	Sound Board
Music History	Stage Lighting
Music History	Stage Mgmt
Music Theory	Studio Arts
Pattern Drafting	Style Versatility
Promotion	Video
Promotion	

Course Descriptions

A well balanced program of general arts studies is one of the many things that sets the Margot Fonteyn Academy of Ballet apart. When Fonteyn developed her plan for the Academy, her idea of balancing ballet training with education in other arts came from her own view that she would have been a much better dancer had she known more about music, art and philosophy. At the Academy, these related subjects make up the course offerings in General Arts Studies.

Below is a list of courses offered in the General Arts curriculum across Lower and Upper School, and Public Ballet, programs.

Anatomy

Professionals will be brought in to teach basic human anatomy, with particular emphasis on how it impacts dance, sport, movement and health. The course will go beyond the mechanical. Skeletal, fluid body, and include neurological systems, viral and bacterial infection, and integration of systems.

Art History

Study of the history of art is the study of human civilization and cultural development throughout recorded time. Beginning with cave paintings and primitive art, students will be brought through each different era of the development of art, including Byzantine, Egyptian, Greek, Roman, Early European, Renaissance, Council of Trent, Baroque, Mannerist, Rococo, Architecture, Realist, Impressionist, Post-Impressionist, Armory Exhibit of 1912, Early American, American Academy, Modern, Post-modern, etc. Lecturers will be brought in from the surrounding area, New York City and beyond to augment these studies. There will also be museum trips associated with these studies.

Basic design

Elements of design in art are universal, and must be understood. Students will begin with basic concepts of light/dark, line, balance, and guiding the eye around the area of the work. From there, they will expand their view to consider color, hue, saturation, perspective, and value. They will study works of fine art, poster art, graphic design for business, fashion, and other areas. All will be viewed from the standpoint of design.

Body Mechanics

Students will explore the mechanical systems of the body as applied to gravity and friction. Working in a basic, elemental way, they will begin to see how the body works to achieve different types of movement, the connection between intention and execution in movement, and how the various laws of physics play out in the body. Examples in this study will include different sports, lifetime activities, as well as popular dance.

Business in Dance

Students will conceive, design, implement and direct a business plan in dance. This may be a student-produced evening of dance, a fundraising drive for a specific dance-related event, use of dance in other charitable fundraising, creating a dance-based product and preparing it for launch, etc. Where possible this will be done in a real-life situation. Professionals will be brought in to lecture on the different aspects of a project's life, and will be sought out as consultants for the particular enterprise the students are involved in. Emphasis will be placed on networking, business relationships in the community, form and function of a Board of Directors, marketing, public relations, demographic identification, and reaching your demographic.

Character Development

Whether in a play, an opera, a ballet or a practice interview, playing a character is the basis for all theatrical stage presentation.

Students learn how to determine the basic qualities of their character, the character's quest, the physical attributes, the back story, and many more details from which to draw in developing an interpretation of a scripted character.

Choreographic Versatility

Professional dancers will be brought in to conduct a series of lecture/demonstration/participation workshops on how the contemporary dancer must be versatile to work in a professional company today. They will be asked to perform different styles of choreography, and to dance a passage in a variety of stylistic ways.

Choreography

Students will begin with Doris Humphrey's "The Art of Making Dances" as a textbook, and then learn the different choreographic skills. They will make their own dances, critique the dances of other students, and view films and video clips of a variety of dance pieces to examine the elements of choreography used.

Color theory

In understanding design, color theory is one of the essentials that demands separate, specific study. They will be taught what makes some colors advance and others recede, and how juxtaposition affects these principles. They will be taught to see what colors are actually there, and how the eye assimilates color and translates it into information beyond simply the way it appears to the eye with normal eyesight.

Composition

Every work of art uses composition, whether it is music, poetry, painting, sculpture, drama, or dance. The basics of composition are as elemental as design and color theory. Students will analyze a variety of compositions and learn how to make a balanced composition without it becoming static. They will learn to look through the lens of a camera, the proscenium of a stage or the boundaries of a canvas and see the composition of the picture within.

Criticism, Critical Review

Art criticism is one of the main avenues of reaching the general public with information about what is happening in the world of the arts. By learning how to look critically at works, the student will learn how to assess their own performance. Criticism here isn't just being negative or finding fault. Instead it is learning how to explain what a person will see or experience when they interact with a specific work of art, what place this work plays in the overall picture of the arts, and their opinion on the quality of that work. They will study reviews of works in the past, and will chronicle current reviews in conjunction with viewing and writing reviews of their own on the same works (movies, restaurants, dances, music recordings, music videos, etc.).

Costuming

When considering dressing dancers, actors or singers, costuming becomes an essential element of design for stage. Students will learn the different types of costuming they can draw from, and how those can be adapted for use on stage. They will learn, and make, the basic elements of costuming (skirts, pants, shirts, dresses/robes and headgear), exploring different types of fabric, cuts and stitches to achieve maximum expression.

Curation

The Academy will have a few gallery spaces where works of visual art will be on display. Students will learn how to select works to display, how to prepare the physical space for display, how to mount the pieces, how to write the exhibition book and how to present individual works in the context of a curated show. They will either organize exhibitions from Mr. Ludden's personal art collection, or find local artists to feature in an exhibition.

Dance History

Using Walter Sorrell's book "Dance Through Time" and the PBS series "The Magic of Dance", students will study all public forms of dance throughout history, and then focusing on the early beginnings of organized theatrical dance in Europe. They will follow the progression of ballerinas from Pavlova to Fracci to Fonteyn to Jamison, on the female side. And they will chart the impact on male dancing Nijinski and Nureyev had, seeing how they laid the foundation for all contemporary dance. They will also study the impact of luminaries such as Balanchine and Baryshnikov. In addition they will study the impact of politics, economics and war on dance.

Eastern Healing

Certified practitioners of various eastern healing traditions will teach the eastern philosophy and approach to the body and to health. This includes the notion of balance being a perpetual state and how syndromes of health are impacted when that balance is disrupted.

Health

Good health is more important than anything else in the life of a dancer. Health professionals will be brought in to lecture on different aspects of health, and teach how to correct, improve and treat different types of common ailments that stand in the way of good health. They will look at diet, environment and stress as elements of health as well, and perform a full health analysis of themselves.

Music (history, analysis, eurhythmics)

Study of music is mandatory throughout the education of Academy students. They will learn basic music theory, and understand that theory in practice. If they are not learning to play a musical instrument (including voice) on their own, then they will study how to read music using a recorder as a means of study and application. They will learn the history of music, the impact of the Age of Reason on the Romantic era, and look at contemporary musical trends, both commercial and classical. They will study the absolute connection between movement and music through the study of eurhythmics.

History of Costume for Ballet

From classic tutu design, through romantic, and ending with the unitard, students will study how costuming in ballet has expanded and limited the range of expression of the choreographer and dancer, and how it has dictated the experience the audience has when viewing performed dance.

History of Costume General

Costumes through the ages have always been an outward expression of the emotional, political, philosophical and psychological nature of our evolving cultures. The study of these costume trends tells the story of human achievement and social development. Students will consider how this impacts their clothing choices today, and the function fashion has on identity and expression. Finally, this will be applied to choices they make when on stage.

Improvisation

Many new dances and dance styles are the result of improvisation. Several choreographers begin working on a new composition with improvisation. Dancers must learn how to dance from the inside out, and how to adapt different movements from the outside in. But in the end, it is the freedom to express and explore in an improvisation that will lead the dancer to integration of expression with maximum movement.

Stage Make-Up

Dancers are expected to do their own stage makeup throughout most of their careers. Only the largest dance companies hire makeup artists to create the characterizations used in ballets, and even then it is only in the story ballets. Since professional dancers are on their own to create their own makeup, they must learn how to do that. They will be taught about different makeup styles, techniques and tools. They will be tested on how to create a makeup plot, as well as on how to execute one. They will also be taught about designing and building facial prosthetics, and basic hair design and implementation.

Music History

Music History is divided into different eras, with particular emphasis on those directly impacting classical ballet. Parallels are drawn to movements in literature and the overall development of society, philosophy, human enterprise and evolving world view.

The ultimate goal is to provide dancers with a clear understanding of any music they might be asked to interpret through choreography, potentially both as a dancer and as a choreographer. Contemporary music, and the various ways music can be used are taught as separate modules of course work.

Music Theory

It is extremely helpful for dancers to be able to read music, understand how and why it is written as it is, and analyze a piece of music. The study of music theory at MFAB is geared toward this approach to music dancers will be asked to interpret through dance and choreography in their careers.

There is a striking parallel between structure of music and structure of choreography. Dance, like music, is an interpretive art form in that the person dancing/playing is giving their own performance perspective to choreography/music developed by someone else.

As dance students grow to understand the underpinnings of the music they are asked to perform to, they will find greater opportunities to shape their interpretation of that music's intent along with that of the choreographer.

Pattern Drafting

Students will learn how to take proper professional measurements, and then how to apply them to create custom fitted costumes. They will learn to work just from a measurement chart, how to alter or adapt prefabricated patterns and how to create pattern pieces from a costume design. They will learn how to create patters using French curls, cutting on the straight and on the bias, how to adjust for different types of fabrics.

Promotion

No matter how good a work of art is, if people don't know it is there, they can't arrange to see it. Promotion is a skill that is as successful as it is refined. Students will learn the different steps one must take to successfully promote something, and also be encouraged to think creatively, stressing that every promotional technique that is recognized today is something that has already been done. It is always the next more creative thing that is the most successful way to promote. In view of this, students will be shown the age old methods while being encouraged to think creatively about promotion.

Public Speaking

When a dancer gets up to speak to the public, it is the same as when silent film stars were suddenly heard for the first time. The public view of a dancer is the view of a silent object, moving beautifully and compellingly through space. One must learn how to speak as eloquently as one moves through ballet choreography. Public speaking will be a skill used by the student for the rest of their life.

Sculpture

Students will be taught additive and subtractive methods for creating three dimensional works of art. They will study the relationship between negative and positive space, how to think in three dimensions, and how elements of design work when brought off of the flat plane. They will study *cire-perdue* casting, clay modeling, kiln firing, glazes, wood carving and construction, mobile and stabile construction, etc.

Set Construction

Carpenters in the ballet and theater worlds are one half of the team that creates the environment in which it all takes place. The construction of scenery and sets is the basis of how the stage "space" is defined. Elements of set design will be studied as well as various techniques for set construction. There will also be study of making, finding, and working with stage props.

Theatrical Backdrop Painting

Painting for stage is an art in itself. Students learn how to develop a color palette that takes into consideration the added visual effects of lighting.

They also learn about scale, how to create depth using vanishing point perspective techniques, and how to create ***trompe d'œil*** architecture, marbled surfaces and many other painterly techniques of the theater.

Scale must be mastered, and techniques for enlarging an exact copy of a rendered backdrop to the vast proportions of stage without distortion are taught. Students take field trips to scene shops and set design studios throughout their time at the Academy.

Ultimately they will have to design stage sets, backdrops, costumes, lighting and choreography with a working knowledge of these techniques and material and labor costs associated with creating new productions.

Sound Board

As symphony orchestras are more unaffordable for live accompaniment in theatrical production, and more types of music are used for the ballet stage, use of a sound board to create the sound element in ballet performance is now essential.

Students will study wiring and configuring a public address system and other components of a sound system, and then how to operate the sound board in live public performance. There will also be instruction for vocal microphones and equalizing and balancing mixed sound between acoustic an digital sound sources.

Stage Lighting

Students will study elements of light for theater, color theory for light, how to create a light plot, and how to design lighting.

They will learn the basic German lighting theories that are commonly used in theater today, but also the lighting theories of the late Vannio Vanni, of the Teatro de La Scalla in Milan, who created a revolutionary type of lighting design in the mid 1970s particularly designed for the ballet stage. This Italian lighting approach is used more and more today and provides the best lighting for dance.

Multiple Emmy Award winner Lincoln Stulik, a member of our Artistic Advisory Committee, is our guest lecturer for this course.

Stage Management

Students will learn how a Stage Manager runs the whole show in a theatrical production. They will learn how to call a show, how to write a cue-by-cue plot sheet, how to integrate load-in, stage setup, lighting focus, setting up light cues on a digital light board, coordination with department heads (electrical, carpentry, light, sound and performers), and how to load out a show.

Studio Arts

Students will learn the basics of drawing, landscape, still life, portraiture and design for drawing. They will keep a portfolio of assigned drawings, as well as a artist's diary, in which they will chronicle their experience during the time of their course in drawings.

The course concludes with a juried public showing of selected works by the students.

Video

Students are taught video camera techniques, lighting for video, storyboarding, how to translate a script into a video shoot, and location management for motion picture production.

They then take the resulting raw footage and learn basic editing techniques – wire frame, compositing, filters, transitions, rendering, and printing to video. In the end they will have a working knowledge of the entire production cycle for video filmmaking.

Dramatic Arts Program

Dancers are always presenting dramatic interpretations of movement, even in abstract pieces. In the story ballets, and even in many short pieces with vivid characters, they must create a character, explore that character's development, and make a statement with their interpretation of that role.

The Dramatic Arts Program is designed to introduce dramatic concepts and techniques to students in the Lower School, and then develop them into professional level skills in the Upper Schools. This involves acting, movement and academic study.

Acting

Each level of both Lower and Upper schools have acting courses offered periodically throughout each year. The training is based on basic skills and exercises to develop dramatic awareness, and ability to express within the context of a character or a scene. Students are eventually given sides to work through, and also develop skills through improvisation.

The acting program spans both Lower and Upper Schools, and students are taught from beginning basic techniques through to development of a character for public performance. In addition to their acting classes, each student is coached on acting in relation to all of their performances for class work, in-Academy performances, Grand Défilée and public performances such as the Nutcracker.

Script Reading

Students learn how to break down a script from different points of view. They answer a set of questions for each scene, from each character's point of view, and then learn how to craft interpretation. They learn how to analyze a script and glean from it the information that is the basis for all interpretation.

Script Writing

Students are led through the process of developing their own script, and then acting the scene they prepare. They are responsible to create dynamic scenes, good dramatic dilemma, clear character identity, and an arch of character development.

Script writing is done in groups initially, so that they learn to assimilate many ideas and benefit from the synergy of the group's dynamics. Each child in the group then works on a specific character to assure differentiation in voice of each character within a script.

Student scripts are prepared and graded, but also rehearsed and performed in the class. Students then critique each other's work, and the performance of that work.

Video

The study of video encompasses all aspects of pre-production, production and post-production for video. Students are walked through each of the departments: photography, sound, light, location, set decoration, etc. and taught from the ground up how to develop an idea into a full video product that can be screened for the public.

They will study under the Technical Director of Nob Hill Video Lab, which is located in the MFAB facilities, as well as with guest instructors.

The study of video also encompasses the study of audio.

Homeschooling Program

The Margot Fonteyn Academy of Ballet offers a program for families who have opted for homeschooling for their children. This program is offered at the Lower School levels 1 and 2 only, and serves children ages 7 through 13. Classes take place between 2:00 and 5:00 pm Monday-Friday, and blended with the normal Saturday schedule for ballet classes.

The Homeschooling Program offers a more intensive General Arts curriculum than the normal Academy student schedule. This is so that homeschooling children who wish to take only General Arts courses can do so without having to fulfill the dance requirements. This General Arts course of study is only offered to children with physiological problems that do not allow them to dance. All other children are required to take the full curriculum that includes classical ballet.

Course Descriptions

Below is a course description of the academic portion of the Homeschooling Program. The weekly ballet class requirements are in addition to this schedule of courses.

Natures I & II

To express one's self through art, it is essential to understand your exact nature. Also, children evolve as they grow and are exposed to different things, and the true nature of each child and his or her gift gradually becomes evident. In view of these facts, MFAB has constructed a course, Natures, which is offered each year. Natures is divided into two parts—The Identity Project, and My Song—that bookend the academic year.

Natures I – "The Identity Project" – is at the beginning of each year. Students learn about the different natures of things (i.e., a book, a dog, a tree, a piano, etc.), and then discover their own natures. During this time they are making drawings of who they feel they are. By the end of the course, they will each have created a visual arts "passport" with the idea that if someone looked at that document, they would know the identity of the person who made it. These visual arts passports are kept from year to year in the students' files.

Natures II – "My Song" – comes at the end of each year. Each child writes a song (lyrics, melody and, for older children, triads to set the key and chord progressions of the song). These songs are then prepared for performance by a professional singer, and a recording is made by that singer of the year's songs. The performance is developed with the student instructing the singer how they want their song performed. The songs are performed by the professional at the Grand Défilé each year.

The cumulative expression of the Nature of each child helps us at MFAB to recognize developmental changes in the child and so better direct their education. This enables us to guide children to develop the talents that are in their best nature to pursue.

General Arts Curriculum

The entire curriculum at MFAB was developed based on Dame Margot Fonteyn's vision that ballet dancers need integrated education in all of the arts related directly to classical ballet. These art forms—Music, Drama and Painting—each have specific methods for being taught and learned.

Through the Lower and Upper schools of the Academy, over the course of a dozen years, there are eight levels; four in each school. We are starting the Homeschooling project with just the first two levels, designed for children ages 8 through 12. It is assumed that each child will be a minimum of two years at each level.

Below are the General Arts courses offered to Homeschoolers at MFAB. Homeschooling Program participants will be placed in accordance to their skill level and maturity. They will take the same entrance placement examination as all Academy candidates, which will determine the appropriate course work for that child.

Level 1

ART

Drawing – Basic drawing begins with shapes, lines, and general composition. The course develops into development of contours, shading and gradient using lines.

Crazy Box – A simple construction of a clay box, using the arbitrary shapes of balls of soft clay rolled flat to create a box and lid. After making several boxes in soft clay, they decide on an approach and create a final project crazy box out of baked clay. Additive and subtractive methods of bas relief are introduced to create decorative elements.

Watercolor – Basic wet-paper watercolor technique is learned, with focus on use of white as an element of composition.

Mono-Prints – starting with “happy accident” work with soft clay, students are taught to see composition elements in random, unplanned compositions. Gradually the elements of composition are explored and students produce a series of mono-prints based on an abstract theme.

What do you see? – Students draw a still life from their point of view, and then practice drawing it from different points of view, eventually attempting to draw from a point of view that is not what they see, but what someone else might see positioned differently.

MUSIC

Rhythm – using claps and stomps (written on staff paper as ‘$_{x}|$’ and ‘$_{o}|$’ respectively) students explore basic rhythm structure. Each student creates a series of claps, stomps and rests to be read and performed by the rest of the class.

Meter – Students learn how to read and construct time signatures, along with incidental markings related to rhythm, meter, tempo and measure demarcation.

Rhythm Composition – Students compose rhythm songs, assigning different percussive instruments made out of materials on hand. Then they learn to play tambourine, maracas, the triangle, and other simple percussion instruments, eventually using them to create compositions that others perform with the composer conducting.

Treble Clef – Notation from middle-C to high-C is learned. Letters for note values are learned, and students “compose” melody strings by writing words using the letters of those note values. The treble clef is introduced, and incidentals relative to it on the musical staff.

Bass Clef – Notation from middle-C to low-C is learned. Letters for note values are learned, and students must transpose the melody strings composed in the Treble Clef class onto the Bass Clef.

DRAMA

Stage Orientation – Students learn the names of the different directional zones of the stage, and the history of theater construction that has dictated those names. They also learn the 8 directions used in classical ballet so that once the direction of "front" is established, all can orient their bodies in the correct directions. They also learn the terms of working on the stage, as well as working back stage and the language that stage management uses to communicate with performers in the dressing room. This is done through creative playing, and then each child creates a mini-scenario and directs the others in it, giving them blocking and basic stage action.

Create Magic – Students are shown a wide variety of stage environments via photographs, sketches, and videos. They discuss what elements create what kind of mood, with inclusion of lighting effects without formal technical lighting terms being used. Then they create magic of their own using what objects, lighting and drapery they have available. They will have a field trip to a theater to see a stage setting up close, and, if possible, will then see a production on that same stage set.

Nutcracker – MFAB students are invited to take part in the Nutcracker performance presented by Les Ballets du Monde, the professional company associated with MFAB. Whether they perform in the production or not, they will learn the different roles (white mice, party children, soldiers, and Mother Ginger's kids) thoroughly, including blocking and simple choreography. Academy students can perform in the production; it is rare that a child does not perform, though it is not required.

Expression – Students learn what posture, countenance, attitude, movement and demeanor constitute different sorts of expression on stage. They practice a wide variety of acting games designed to hone their ability to get into character, develop the character, and perform in such a way that they will be understood in a large theater.

Who/What am I? – Students invent characters, animals, and fantasy objects and alien beings. They are encouraged to include props and costume elements. They work to create clear portrayals that the other students and the faculty members can identify.

Character Sketch – As a final acting project, each child creates a Character Sketch to be performed at the Grand Défilé. The Grand Défilé scores count for 1/3 of their overall grade for the year.

Level 2

MUSIC 1

Note Value – Students learn and understand note value in general. They explore the various ways notation depicts value, dynamic and meter, and learn what individual notes and rests look like on and off of the staff.

Treble Scale – Students learn the treble clef Cmaj scale, and are introduced to flats and sharps.

Bass Scale – Students learn the bass clef Cmaj scale, and are introduced to flats and sharps.

Composition – Students learn basic Sonata-Allegro form of composition, and its variants (cannon, Passacaglia, Theme and Variations). They then listen to a wide variety of recorded music to identify the different sorts of compositional elements and forms. They also learn the standard Verse-Chorus structure of traditional, folk, popular and commercial music.

Lyrics – Students go through the process of developing lyrics, while studying the form of lyrics to songs they know.

MUSIC 2

Incidentals – Here students learn the written language of music, and how to talk about details when discussing performance of any piece of written music. First they learn the various means of notating the music itself, and the specifics of how it is to be performed. We touch on dynamic markings, however, students are only exposed so that as they look at a musical score they know what sort of thing each element is. This universally applied language of dynamic is largely in Italian; students are not required to know these words, but they fall into the category of extra credit if learned. Dynamics are taught at Level 3.

Meter/Rhythm – Students compose rhythmic studies in various meters to be played by other students. Then they compose for more than one instrument (tambourine, hand claps, triangle, tom-tom, etc.) and learn how to write a simple conductor's score, and to create a score for each instrument. They ultimately create rhythmic studies that will be performed by small groups of students with the composer conducting.

Simple Songs 1 – Students learn the history of songs as means of recording history, teaching myth, honoring events and individuals, and entertaining.

Simple Songs 2 – Students learn the history of songs as means of recording history, teaching myth, honoring events and individuals, and entertaining.

ART

Baked Clay – Students make an abstract design that will be turned into a three-dimensional clay sculpture using a wire armature.

Positive/Negative Space – Students observe a wide range of sculptures, exploring the negative and positive space, with particular attention to the interplay between the two. They also look at the human form in motion to see how negative and positive space can be used to communicate to the audience. They study photographs, actual sculptures, primitive art forms, and use their own bodies to create positive and negative space ideas and dialogs with the viewer.

Vanishing Point – Simple perspective is studied, both in existing works of art, photographs, and the real world around us. Then this study is applied to paper through pencil drawing. Volumetric perspective is introduced and students draw architectural forms and organic forms applying this knowledge.

Light Box 1 & 2 – This course is in several steps. The students ultimately create a papier-maché box on which the exterior sides each depict a work of art in a series (the four seasons, a rainbow, a day at the amusement park, waking up, sun and moon cycles, etc.). These depictions are created with tissue paper decoupage and colored pencil drawing. It is called a Light Box, because the under-structure is painted pure gesso white, and the light then shows through the tissue paper being illuminated by the light reflecting off of the under surface.

DRAMA

Enter the Stage – Students learn how to enter the stage, walk, and establish character, mood, and atmosphere.

Stage Make-Up – Students learn to create a masque foundation, and then visually sculpt protrusion, cavity and swelling with make-up. They start by creating a believable bruise. They simultaneously learn how to make a formal Make-Up Plot, and then how to turn that into an actual made up actor on a stage. They work from photographs of theater and in fashion magazines, and progress to completely original, invented make-up for characters they also create.

Nutcracker – MFAB students are invited to take part in the Nutcracker performance presented by Les Ballets du Monde, the professional company associated with MFAB. Whether they perform in the production or not, they will learn the different roles (white mice, party children, soldiers, and Mother Ginger's kids) thoroughly, including blocking and simple choreography. Academy students can perform in the production; it is rare that a child does not perform, though it is not required.

Script Reading – Students are presented with scripts from scenes with which they may be familiar, and learn how to dissect the script from each character's point of view. Then they move to scripts with which they are unfamiliar and must find the character motivation, back-story elements, overall scene definition, and movement for each character in the scene.

Script Writing – Students work in teams to write a script that includes them all, and then perform that script. Student scripts are performed in the classroom at the end of the course, but the best script will be performed at the Grand Défilé.

Character Development – Students learn how to create a character, establish back-story, and to incorporate character traits (physical, kinetic and emotional). They do exercises for getting into character, and then practice staying in character no matter what distractions there might be.

SCHOLARLY ARTS

Introduction to Art History – Students begin with cave painting, learning where the first and oldest forms of art are found in the world, and what they depict. They move from there through the development of art forms through the ancient Greek empire. This introduces the concept of mythology, of which there is some discussion geared toward the study of mythology in art that comes later in their studies at Level 2.

Art in Time – Students learn the cyclical development of art trends through history (cartoon, realism, mannerism, surrealism, abstraction, cartoon…). Then they look at random works of art and determine where they fall within the cycle of development in their time. They then are introduced to major identifying characteristics of the main periods of art history (Greek, Roman, Byzantine, Pre-Raphaelite, Renaissance, High Renaissance, Early Baroque, Baroque, Rococo, Impressionism, Post-Impressionism, and Expressionism). They are not expected to know these eras, but the familiarity with the imagery is the basis of future exploration in art history studies at higher levels.

Early Music – Music that has survived from before notation, or in early forms of notation is studied. The relative pitch of 5ths is introduced, versus the relative pitch of octaves we use today. They listen to different types of early music from cultures all over the world, and are exposed to the idea that there are many different types of scales and note intervals used in different cultures.

Folk Music – Troubadours were the news magazines of their time, and folk music knitted societal culture together before electricity. Students study the place of folk music in cultural life, and how it works to shore up a community. This was the basis for liturgical music, and lead to the development of hymns. In folk and church music the performer stands behind the song, as the meaning of the music and lyrics is far more important than the personality or facility of the performer. This humility in musical form is then followed to today's music traditions and identified.

Fashion – The history of how people dress, and why, is studied. The invention of neck ties, hoop skirts, bustles, cuff buttons, cummerbunds, snoods, ruffles, fans, capes, muffs and more are each the result of very practical needs of the time. Students learn how these developed, and what different forms they take in every day attire. They then look at traditional dress in foreign cultures and see how these same human issues have guided the development of fashion throughout human history.

History of Costume – Stage costuming is an art form that is very complex, but can be seen in clear, direct developmental terms. Students study the nature, function, place and purpose of stage costumes, and follow their development through modern history.

Index

www.ingramcontent.com/pod-product-compliance
Ingram Content Group UK Ltd.
Pitfield, Milton Keynes, MK11 3LW, UK
UKHW020219250726
13967UKWH00001B/77

9 781105 626043